PLAYS OF SCIENCE & INVENTION

21 FASCINATING SCENES FOR THE CLASSROOM OR STAGE

By THOMAS H

MERIWETHER PUBLISHING
A division of Pioneer Drama Service, Inc.
Denver, Colorado

Meriwether Publishing
A division of Pioneer Drama Service, Inc.
PO Box 4267
Englewood, CO 80155-4267

www.pioneerdrama.com

© Copyright 2021 Meriwether Publishing

Printed in the United States of America
First Edition

All rights are strictly reserved, including professional, motion picture, radio, broadcasting, television, video or sound taping, all other forms of mechanical or electronic reproductions such as information storage and retrieval systems and photocopying, and the rights of translation into foreign languages. Any inquiries concerning these rights should be directed to the publisher at the address above.

The rights to unlimited amateur performances of these plays at one location are granted with the purchase of this book. For performances at another location, a royalty fee of $10 per play per performance must be remitted to Pioneer Drama Service, Inc. using the form on page 184 of this book.

Amateur groups are permitted to make small changes to language or abridge a play for contest purposes, provided that the playwright's intent remains intact. Any inquiries concerning changes should be directed to the publisher.

Permission to reproduce cast copies of individual plays included in this text is granted to amateur groups with the purchase of this book. Copies of these plays and amateur performance rights are for the purchaser and purchasing organization only. These rights may not be sold or transferred to any third party.

ISBN: 978-1-56608-266-2

Library of Congress Control Number: 2021935957

CONTENTS

Acknowledgements vi

Preface vii

240 BC - Footsteps Around the World (3M) 1
Greek mathematician and astronomer Eratosthenes tries to convince Egyptian Pharaoh Ptolemy III that Earth is not flat.

1250 - Miracle Glass (1M, 3F) 9
A medieval glass craftsman, working on a panel of stained glass for the Siena Cathedral, discovers that objects are magnified when viewed through curved pieces of clear glass, a concept that would lead to the earliest form of eyeglasses.

1519 - Mirror Image Scribbling (2M) 17
After the death of Leonardo da Vinci, his pupil Francesco Melzi defends his teacher's anatomical drawings and mechanical sketches to a skeptical French aristocrat who values da Vinci only as an artist.

1529 - The Mad Prophet of Medicine (2M, 3F) 25
The itinerant physician Paracelsus is scorned by the medical community because of his radical ideas about the source of disease coming from outside the body and not by unbalanced "humours" within.

1634 - And Yet It Moves (2M, 2F) 33
The aged Galileo Galilei, put under house arrest by the Pope for his heretical ideas about Earth revolving around the sun, is visited by his two children, who smuggle out some of their father's manuscripts to be published abroad.

1795 - To Frame My Face (1M, 2F) 43
An aristocratic French lady who survived smallpox is scarred for life and finds a new identity as a cabaret singer disguised under stage makeup.

1833 - Noise (2M, 2F) 51
Inspired by the electromagnetic system invented by Charles Thomas Jackson, acclaimed painter Samuel Morse turns to science and invents a telegraph device.

1876 - Words and Wires (2M, 2F) 59
Inventor Alexander Graham Bell is studying the transmission of sound with his assistant Thomas A. Watson when they stumble onto the basis for the telephone.

1896 - No Wires (3M, 1F) 67
Young Italian inventor Guglielmo Marconi and his mother arrive in England to get funding from the British Admiralty for Marconi's new wireless radio transmission system.

1901 - The Train to Tuskegee (2M, 1F) 75
Black agricultural scientist George Washington Carver, waiting for a train with a White farming couple, enlightens them on how to improve the productivity of their cotton farm.

1914 - Little Curies (2M, 2F) 83
During World War I, Marie Curie and her daughter Irene struggle to get mobile X-ray machines to surgeons treating wounded soldiers at front-line hospitals in France.

1925 - King of the Universe (2M, 2F) 91
The young British-American astronomer Cecilia Payne goes against conventional scientific thinking when she determines that the sun is composed mostly of hydrogen, getting resistance from an older, renowned Princeton astronomer.

1928 - Mold Juice (2M, 2F) 101
Doctor and scientist Alexander Fleming returns from vacation to find mold growing in one of his Petri dishes containing a staph culture, leading him to the discovery of penicillin.

1939 - Garage Guys (2M, 1F) 111
Bill Hewlett and David Packard, electrical engineers who met while attending Stanford University, form the innovative electronics company Hewlett-Packard on New Year's Day in Packard's garage.

1942 - The Movie Star and the Composer (3M, 1F) 119
Hollywood beauty Hedy Lamarr and avant-garde composer George Antheil present an ingenious plan to confuse and disable enemy radio torpedoes, but the U.S. Navy refuses to take them seriously.

1944 - Decoding the Doll Woman (2M, 1F) 127
Renowned cryptologist Elizebeth Smith Friedman helps the FBI close in on a spy who was using her antique doll shop in New York City as a means of passing on vital information about U.S. Naval ships to the Japanese.

1951 - Feeding the Enemy (1M, 1F) 137
The Black biochemist Jane C. Wright explains to Louis Tompkins Wright, her father and the director of the Harlem Hospital Research Center, that she may have found a way to make chemotherapy effective in destroying cancer cells.

1962 - No More Birdsong (1M, 3F) 145
Nature author and environmentalist Rachel Carson, in the hospital for cancer treatments, sees the publication of her book *Silent Spring* threatened by big chemical companies who want to keep the truth about harmful pesticides from reaching the public.

1982 - Magic Rings (1M, 2F) 155
A retired science teacher who has studied Saturn all his life is thrilled to see the first up-close photos of the planet taken by the space probe Voyager 1.

1999 - The Millennium Bug (1M, 2F) 165
As midnight approaches on New Year's Eve before the new millennium, two astronomy professors and a student are in the college planetarium to see what effect Y2K will have on the computer that operates the star presentation.

2021 AD/391 BC - Modern Medical Advice (2M, 2F)...... 173
A twenty-first-century doctor examines her middle-aged male patient, while Greek physician Hippocrates examines a middle-aged patient in his medical school. Both patients have similar ailments, and both doctors use Hippocrates's timeless approach to medical practice.

Appendix - Plays by Branch of Science 182

About the Author 183

Performance Application 184

ACKNOWLEDGEMENTS

I am indebted to a pair of Wolfs in helping make these plays scientifically accurate and competently literate: Dr. Larry L. Wolf and Dr. Janet Wolf. A hearty "thank you" also to three Sanders—Robert, Jackie, and Dorothy—as well as to Mark Robinson, and to my wife, Cathy, who were the readers who allowed me to hear the plays aloud and to benefit from their acting and comments.

PREFACE

This anthology of short plays is a sequel of sorts to *Plays of the American Experience: 25 Fascinating Plays for the Stage* (Meriwether Publishing, 2018). While that anthology concentrated on American history between 1845 and 1973, this collection has an international scope and consists of short plays dealing with science and scientists. It goes as far back as the ancient world and continues into the age of computers and advanced technology. Various fields of science—from physics and medicine to astronomy and cryptology—are explored, and both famous and undeservedly neglected men and women of science are included.

As with the anthology of short works about history, *Plays of Science & Invention* seeks to humanize a subject that is too often a matter of cold hard facts. Plays are about people; science is not people. Yet all scientific breakthroughs and discoveries were made by men and women who went beyond what was only previously observed, if noticed at all. And most science affects all people, be it through areas of study as different as medicine and modern communications. The goal here is to make important scientific ideas and notable scientists more real by dramatizing them.

Also similar to the previous anthology, plays run between eight and ten minutes long with a cast size of two to five characters per play, and have simple costume, prop, and set requirements. This will allow them to be produced easily in a classroom or on stage. The detailed set descriptions and stage directions are included to help the actors visualize the scene and are not meant as production demands. Just having the plays read aloud will prove effective in a school classroom. Presenting the plays for other students, or staged in competitions or for the community, would be even more effective.

Before each play is a "Background" section which gives information about the scientist, that particular aspect of science, or the historical context of the drama to follow. Most of the characters are real people unless indicated otherwise in the character listing. Following each play is an "Aftermath" that explains what happened after the events of the drama. The "Background" and "Aftermath" sections are not only for teaching purposes but also for young actors and other readers to better understand how the play fits into history and the world of science.

I have been very pleased with the many comments and compliments regarding *Plays of the American Experience* and how I was able to make history come alive for students. It is my hope that I will be able to do the same with the widely varied field of science.

FOOTSTEPS AROUND THE WORLD
(240 BC)

BACKGROUND

Eratosthenes of Cyrene is considered the "father of geography," but he was also a celebrated mathematician, astronomer, poet, and chronologist. Born in 276 BC in the Greek city of Cyrene in North Africa, Eratosthenes was educated in Athens. He first found fame as a poet and a chronicler of Greek and Egyptian history. At just 30 years old, Eratosthenes was chosen by the Egyptian pharaoh Ptolemy III Euergetes to work at the renowned Library of Alexandria. By 240 BC, Eratosthenes was chief librarian and tutor to the pharaoh's sons. During this time, he pursued his interests in mathematics and astronomy and, using both fields of study, made several remarkable discoveries in geography.

CHARACTERS

PHILOPATOR (M) ....Ptolemy's eldest child; twelve years old
PTOLEMY III (M) ....Pharaoh of Egypt
ERATOSTHENES
   OF CYRENE (M) ....Greek geographer, mathematician, and astronomer

SETTING

Time: June 26, 240 BC. Late afternoon.
Place: A room in the pharaoh's palace in Alexandria, Egypt.

SET DESCRIPTION

The private room in the palace has an elaborate chair for the pharaoh, but it is not a throne. There is no other furniture.

LIGHTS UP on the room in Pharaoh's palace. PTOLEMY paces back and forth restlessly as young PHILOPATOR stands by nervously. Both are dressed casually.

PHILOPATOR: Perhaps I should have said nothing, Father. I am sorry.

PTOLEMY: You did the right thing, child. When I ask you what Eratosthenes taught you today, you must answer me honestly.

PHILOPATOR: Maybe I heard incorrectly. Maybe he didn't say that at all. Maybe it was something completely different and I got it mixed up.

PTOLEMY: The son of the pharaoh does not get mixed up!

PHILOPATOR: No, Father. *(Pause.)* You aren't going to scold Master Eratosthenes, are you, Father?

PTOLEMY: You can't scold a Greek. You always end up getting into a metaphysical debate! They're incorrigible!

PHILOPATOR: You won't throw him to the crocodiles, will you?

PTOLEMY: What good would that do? He would talk the poor creatures to abstraction!

PHILOPATOR: I'm so glad. Besides, who else could run the Library of Alexandria like Master Eratosthenes?

PTOLEMY: I've no objection to the man as a librarian. He's brilliant! It's been less than a year since I put him in charge of the library, and he has done some commendable things.

PHILOPATOR: Like the chronology of Egyptian kings! Last week, we went through it together. It names and dates every king of the land going back to—

PTOLEMY: Yes, yes. All very impressive.

PHILOPATOR: Your name is there, Father!

PTOLEMY: I should hope so.

PHILOPATOR: And your father's and his father's and—

PTOLEMY: It is a remarkable piece of work.

PHILOPATOR: And do you know what Master Eratosthenes is having the scribes do now?

PTOLEMY: What is that?

PHILOPATOR: They are writing a duplicate copy of every book in the library!

PTOLEMY: Every book? Whatever for?

PHILOPATOR: Master Eratosthenes says that many books have been lost over the years. People borrow the books, and they are never returned.

PTOLEMY: *(Explodes.)* Outrageous! Who are these people?

PHILOPATOR: Mostly members of the royal family.

PTOLEMY: *(Backs down.)* Well... I will have to look into that.

PHILOPATOR: The scribes are excellent men, Father. Master Eratosthenes showed me some of the duplicates and they are even more beautifully written than the originals! And do you know what happens to the duplicates, Father?

PTOLEMY: Stored with the originals, I imagine.

PHILOPATOR: Not at all. They are kept in a completely different part of the library. That way, if there is ever a fire in one part of the building and the other parts are saved, the books will not be lost forever.

PTOLEMY: A fire in the Library of Alexandria! The very idea! But duplicating every book in the library? That will take... years!

PHILOPATOR: Six years, three months, and seventeen days.

PTOLEMY: What?

PHILOPATOR: Master Eratosthenes calculated the length of time it will take.

PTOLEMY: Those Greeks do like their numbers. But they also have the craziest ideas! Like what you told me today! And Eratosthenes and his obsession with spheres! "The moon is a sphere and the sun is a sphere, so Earth must be a sphere." I've heard the speech a dozen times!

PHILOPATOR: Master Eratosthenes teaches that the shape of Earth was determined long before he was born and is now generally accepted by scholars.

PTOLEMY: *(Scoffs.)* Greek scholars! Here in Egypt, I am content to be on level ground and not let the Nile flow up the side of a sphere!

PHILOPATOR: Father, I see Master Eratosthenes coming!

PTOLEMY: And about time, too!

PHILOPATOR: Please, don't be angry, Father. And please don't feed him to the crocodiles!

PTOLEMY: Hush, child. *(Sits in the chair.)* Do not speak unless I ask you to.

PHILOPATOR: Yes, Father.

ERATOSTHENES: *(Casually ENTERS wearing simple clothes and bows to PTOLEMY.)* Your Highness, the Pharaoh of All the Land...

PTOLEMY: You are late. How far can it be from the library to the palace?

ERATOSTHENES: Are you in earnest, my Pharaoh?

PTOLEMY: I am always in earnest.

ERATOSTHENES: Then I will tell you. It is exactly 432 cubits from the steps of the library to the entrance to the palace. I counted on my way here.

PTOLEMY: Why would you do that?

ERATOSTHENES: Natural curiosity.

PTOLEMY: Greek curiosity, you mean. And just how did you determine that length? Did you use a measuring stick as you walked?

ERATOSTHENES: Not necessary, my Pharaoh. I calculated that my footstep at a casual pace is equal to two-point-four cubits. So, by counting my footsteps—

PTOLEMY: No wonder you are late. You should have planned on coming to your pharaoh at a much faster pace! My child tells me you discussed the shape of Earth again today.

ERATOSTHENES: Oh, we talked about much more beyond the mere shape of Earth.

PTOLEMY: You know my feelings about a spherical Earth?

ERATOSTHENES: Indeed, I do, my Pharaoh. But as young Philopator here will one day be pharaoh in a generally accepted spherical world, I thought it best—

PTOLEMY: You thought?! You thought! That's the trouble with you Greeks! You're always thinking!

ERATOSTHENES: *(Bows.)* It is a national handicap.

PTOLEMY: According to my child, who I trust and believe implicitly, you not only insist on the... roundness of this world, but you actually claim to have determined how big this sphere is!

ERATOSTHENES: That is correct, my Pharaoh.

PTOLEMY: How was this accomplished? Did you walk around the sphere and count your footsteps?

ERATOSTHENES: I fear Earth is far too large for such an approach.

PTOLEMY: Not to mention the problem of walking right off the edge and into the abyss. My child also tells me that you calculated this extremely large measurement rather recently.

ERATOSTHENES: Five days ago, my Pharaoh, on the summer solstice.

PTOLEMY: No doubt you needed a very long day to figure it out.

ERATOSTHENES: I needed to wait for the solstice in order to get my final calculations. Perhaps young Philopator can tell you what I explained to him today?

PTOLEMY: *(To PHILOPATOR.)* Can you?

PHILOPATOR: I... I can try...

PTOLEMY: It is not necessary. *(To ERATOSTHENES.)* I do not wish to hear my own child spouting off your cockeyed ideas.

PHILOPATOR: But, Father—!

PTOLEMY: *(Scolds.)* Philopator! *(Pause.)*

ERATOSTHENES: If you will allow me, my Pharaoh, I will explain what I have done. All that I ask is that you oblige me with the... fiction that the world is a sphere. If you can sustain such a pretense, I think I can describe today's lesson.

PTOLEMY: I smell Greek trickery at work here...

ERATOSTHENES: What you will. Now, the only accurate way to measure a sphere is to determine its circumference. If one can calculate the length of a line that encircles a sphere at its widest point, it is possible to find out the size and even the volume of it.

PTOLEMY: How is that possible?

ERATOSTHENES: Through mathematics. The circle consists of 360 degrees, so—

PTOLEMY: Yes, yes. I understand all that. But you are getting away from my question. In what manner have you supposedly measured the size of Earth?

ERATOSTHENES: Walking around the Earth at its widest point and measuring it, we have agreed, is impractical.

PTOLEMY: Not to mention ridiculous.

ERATOSTHENES: And ridiculous. All the tools we need to measure the Earth are in the sky. Specifically, the sun.

PTOLEMY: Go easy, Eratosthenes. As pharaoh, I have a special relationship with the sun.

ERATOSTHENES: Which will make this calculation all the more important to you, my Pharaoh. *(To PHILOPATOR.)* And to you, young Philopator.

PTOLEMY: Go on...

ERATOSTHENES: One year ago, I went to Swenett, which lies 72 leagues north of us. When the sun was directly overhead on the summer solstice, I took a rod 57 cubits long and placed it vertically into the ground. Measuring the length of the shadow it cast, I was in fact measuring a triangle and was able to determine the angle of the sun's rays. Five days ago, I repeated the same experiment here in Alexandria. Knowing the distance from Swenett to Alexandria allowed me to create another triangle with an angle of seven degrees. Using geometry of parallel lines, the distance from Alexandria to Swenett must be 7/360th the total circumference of Earth. Thus, I was able to figure out the complete length of the circle. In other words, the measurement of Earth's circumference.

PTOLEMY: And how many cubits was it?

ERATOSTHENES: A cubit is much too small a unit for such a great distance. I translated the numbers to rods and then to leagues. The circumference of Earth is 4,390 leagues.

PTOLEMY: That is outrageous! The distance to Persia and back is about six hundred leagues. You are saying that the Earth is... is...?

ERATOSTHENES: Is much larger than we ever imagined. Our world here is just a small corner of a very big sphere.

PHILOPATOR: Isn't it astounding, Father?

PTOLEMY: Hush, son... *(Contemplates.)* Eratosthenes...

ERATOSTHENES: Yes, my Pharaoh?

PTOLEMY: You are a very brilliant... very dangerous man.

PHILOPATOR: Father?

PTOLEMY: Eratosthenes, you must not breathe a word of this to anyone. It will cause... chaos!

ERATOSTHENES: Nothing has changed, my Pharaoh. Everything is as it was. Only now, we know more.

PTOLEMY: You know more! And I want you to keep it to yourself!

ERATOSTHENES: Egypt is the same vast empire it always was. Its size and power have not changed. Your position and power have not changed.

PTOLEMY: But if you are right—and of course you cannot be right—then I am not pharaoh of most of the world!

ERATOSTHENES: You command most of the known world, my Pharaoh. No one is much concerned with the unknown world. It may all be a vast wasteland.

PTOLEMY: I order you, Eratosthenes, to keep your crazy numbers and triangles and conclusions to yourself! They are dangerous ideas.

ERATOSTHENES: I will deposit my notes deep in the archives of the library, and no one will take notice of them. They may prove useful to future generations.

PTOLEMY: I'd prefer it if you would burn them.

PHILOPATOR: No, Father!

ERATOSTHENES: Even if I did, my Pharaoh, the fact remains. We live on a very large planet.

PTOLEMY: Large or not, no one has any business knowing its size!

ERATOSTHENES: *(Smiles.)* If you don't tell anyone, I promise to remain silent. *(Bows.)*

PTOLEMY: That's more like it.

ERATOSTHENES: Of course, I cannot speak for the young Philopator. Good day, Your Highness, Pharaoh of all the land. *(EXITS.)*

PTOLEMY: *(Thinks.)* Cannot speak for Philopator? *(Calls OFF.)* What do you mean by that? *(To PHILOPATOR.)* What did he mean by that?

PHILOPATOR: *(Smiles.)* I cannot say, Father.

PTOLEMY: Arrrgh! I should have fed him to the crocodiles! *(LIGHTS FADE to BLACK.)*

AFTERMATH

Eratosthenes's calculated circumference of Earth—translated to modern measurements—was 46,100 kilometers or 27,400 miles. Though the distance from Swenett to Alexandria was inaccurately measured at the time, he was off by only 15 percent. (Earth is actually 40,075 kilometers or 24,900 miles in circumference.) Eratosthenes remained in Alexandria for the rest of his long life. Among his many accomplishments were calculating the tilt of the Earth's axis, determining the distance from the Earth to the sun, making the first known map of Earth as a global projection with longitude and latitude lines, and coming up with the mathematical algorithm known as the Sieve of Eratosthenes, which is used for finding prime numbers. At the age of 80, Eratosthenes gradually went blind and, in 194 BC, he committed suicide by starving himself to death. Parts of the Library of Alexandria were accidentally burned by Julius Caesar and his Roman troops in 48 BC.

MIRACLE GLASS
(1250)

BACKGROUND

It is not known who invented eyeglasses or even who first found that curved glass created a form of lens. The craftsmen who most worked with glass in the Middle Ages were those unknown artists who made the stained glass windows for churches and cathedrals. Because the word "lens" probably comes from the Italian "lente di vetro," the seed plant known as a "glass lentil," it is likely that the first lens was made in Italy. The seed of the "glass lentil" resembles an eyeglass lens. Such an unscientific way of naming the invention suggests that it was not made by a physician or scientist. By 1300, there are records of eyeglasses being made and used.

CHARACTERS*

ENZO (M)..................................glass craftsman
GABRIELLA (F).......................his wife
DANIELA (F)............................Enzo and Daniela's fourteen-year-old daughter
NONNA (F)...............................Gabriella's mother

*ALL characters are fictional

SETTING

Time: A sunny Sunday afternoon in May 1250.
Place: Enzo's glass workshop in Siena, Italy.

SET DESCRIPTION

The workshop is in the front room of the house and has two windows with shutters but no glass. A large worktable has the lead and the stained glass that ENZO is working on. There is at least one piece of flat glass and one piece of curved glass. Also on the table are drawings on paper and tools such as a chisel, file, mallet, small saw, etc. There is a shelf filled with rolled-up drawings. At the table are two wooden stools. A doorway leads to the rest of the house.

PROPERTIES

Walking stick (NONNA).

LIGHTS UP on Enzo's workshop. The shutters are open and the afternoon sun fills the room with light. ENZO works, hunched over the table, filing a piece of clear glass as DANIELA leans with her elbows on the table, watching him closely.

DANIELA: How come that piece of glass has no color, Papa?

ENZO: This piece? *(Holds it up to the light.)* Why, Daniela, this little piece has the most color of all!

DANIELA: But it is clear. I can see right through it. No color.

ENZO: Here in my shop, it may seem so. But once it is part of the window in the cathedral, it will have many colors!

DANIELA: How is that possible? *(ENZO laughs.)* Papa, you are teasing me!

ENZO: I speak the truth. This clear piece of glass is going to be part of the halo of St. Cecilia. At dawn, the little piece of glass will be yellow from the rising sun. In the heat of the day, the bright sun will make it seem almost white. At sunset the glass will be a lovely orange. And at night, if the moon is bright enough, it will be a blue white. So many colors in one piece of clear glass!

DANIELA: *(Picks up a green piece of glass.)* But this piece will only be green?

ENZO: It, too, will change with the light, but yes, Daniela, it will always be green.

DANIELA: I wish I could be a glass craftsman someday, Papa!

ENZO: Don't let your mother hear you speak such nonsense. It is a man's profession, Daniela. You know that.

DANIELA: But I want to make beautiful things out of glass like you do!

ENZO: Instead you will make beautiful children. That, no man can do. *(Resumes working.)*

DANIELA: But what if all my babies are ugly?

ENZO: Don't talk foolishness, Daniela. My daughter will have beautiful children. Look at your mamma. Lovely still!

DANIELA: Look at Nonna! What if my children look like Nonna?

ENZO: Your grandmother is well over 60!

DANIELA: No teeth and nearly blind.

ENZO: Your children will have teeth and good eyes. *(Holds up the glass.)* There! I think I have the curve just right. *(Hands it to DANIELA.)*

DANIELA: It is so smooth and round! How do you do that, Papa?

ENZO: If the glass is strong and has no flaws, it is possible to cut away the edges and make it curved. In the window, it will stand out from the flat glass. Perfect for St. Cecilia's halo!

GABRIELLA: *(ENTERS through the doorway, wearing an apron, a scarf over her hair, and a necklace with a cross.)* Daniela! There you are! How many times have I told you Papa's workshop is no place for a young signora?

DANIELA: I like to watch Papa work. *(Plays with the piece of glass, looking through it and turning it about.)*

GABRIELLA: You'll get a speck of glass in your eye and squint the rest of your life! Who will marry you then? Enzo, it is Sunday. What if the priest walks by and sees you working on the holy day? He'll threaten you with everlasting damnation!

ENZO: If I don't deliver this panel to the foreman by sunrise on Tuesday, he will threaten much worse. You want to eat, don't you?

GABRIELLA: Close the shutters then!

ENZO: If I close the shutters, I will be in the dark. Do you know what stained glass looks like in the dark? No color. All black.

GABRIELLA: You have an answer for everything! A wife can lose her mind with such a stubborn man! Come, Daniela, we need to make the sauce! *(Starts to leave.)*

ENZO: *(Smiles.)* Making the sauce on the holy day? What would the priest say?

GABRIELLA: *(Turns back.)* You want to eat, don't you?

ENZO: *(Laughs.)* Now look who has all the answers!

GABRIELLA: Come, Daniela, you heard me! *(EXITS as DANIELA holds the piece of clear glass up to the light coming from the window.)*

DANIELA: This curved glass—the clear piece—it is all white.

ENZO: That is because the sun is high in the sky. *(Starts filing another piece of glass.)* You'd better do what your mamma tells you, Daniela.

DANIELA: *(Moves the piece of glass around to examine an object.)* But when I look far way, objects are not clear anymore. They are all blurry. It makes me dizzy.

ENZO: That is because it is curved. The light gets all mixed up.

DANIELA: But, Papa... *(Holds the glass about a foot above the tabletop and looks at one of the drawings.)* If I look through the glass like this, this picture appears very clear. The glass makes things big.

ENZO: *(Concentrating on his work.)* What do you mean it makes things big?

DANIELA: *(Takes the glass away from her eye.)* If I look at one of your drawings of St. Cecilia, she is little. You can see her in only one corner of the window, very small.

ENZO: That is because it is a very large window. In the actual panel, she will be bigger.

DANIELA: I understand that, Papa. *(Peers through the glass.)* But when I look at St. Cecilia through your curved glass, she is not so little. The glass makes her bigger.

ENZO: *(Stops working.)* You are talking nonsense. Let me see. *(Goes to DANIELA and she hands him the glass.)*

DANIELA: Hold the glass like this, Papa. *(Demonstrates.)* Now look...

ENZO: I don't understand it... *(Looks though the glass, then looks at the drawing without the glass. He is puzzled and thinks a moment, then repeats the process.)*

DANIELA: And look at this, Papa. *(Takes the glass from him.)* If I hold the glass very close to St. Cecilia, she is the same size as the drawing. *(Demonstrates.)* But the more I move the glass away from her, the bigger she gets!

ENZO: Let me try that. *(Takes the glass from her and repeats the movement.)* This is something very strange...

DANIELA: Do you think it is dark magic, Papa? Perhaps the devil is in the glass and—!

ENZO: No, no, my child! There must be a logical reason for this. And it must have something to do with the curve of the glass. *(Takes another piece of glass and looks at the drawing.)* It does not happen with the flat piece of glass. It must be the curve! *(DANIELA takes the glass from him as GABRIELLA ENTERS.)*

GABRIELLA: Daniela, didn't you hear what I told you?

ENZO: Gabriella, come here and look at this!

DANIELA: Mamma, it is the most amazing thing!

GABRIELLA: *(Crosses to DANIELLA.)* Take that glass away from your eye, Daniela! *(Takes the glass.)* It is too dangerous! I don't want you coming in the workshop again!

ENZO: But look through the glass, Gabriella!

GABRIELLA: I will do no such thing! *(Puts it down on the table.)* Come, Daniela! The sauce!

ENZO: Then I will show you. *(Picks up the glass.)* Come and sit here, Gabriella.

GABRIELLA: Enzo! Stop this foolishness!

ENZO: *(Commands.)* Sit! *(GABRIELLA reluctantly sits.)* Do you see this sketch of St. Cecilia?

GABRIELLA: Of course I can see it! I have eyes!

ENZO: Now look at St. Cecilia through this glass... *(Holds the glass above the sketch.)* Now what do you see?

GABRIELLA: *(Dismissively.)* St. Cecilia!

DANIELA: But, Mamma, she is bigger!

ENZO: And as I move the glass closer to your eyes—

DANIELA: She gets even bigger!

GABRIELLA: *(Rises and moves away from the table, frightened.)* This is some kind of black magic! Enzo, what have you done?!

DANIELA: Papa says it's not black magic—

ENZO: Of course not! It is just curved glass. Not magic.

GABRIELLA: But it does such strange things to the eyes!

ENZO: I should have noticed it a long time ago. Daniela saw it first—

GABRIELLA: Daniela! You must not speak of this! People will think you are working with the devil!

DANIELA: The devil!

ENZO: Don't talk such nonsense. You are frightening the girl.

GABRIELLA: No good could come from this... this...

ENZO: *(Gets excited.)* This little miracle of glass! Don't you see? If the curved glass can make things appear larger, then the eye can see more!

GABRIELLA: If God wanted us to see more, He would have given us bigger eyes!

DANIELA: I just thought of something, Papa! I will be right back! *(Runs OUT.)*

GABRIELLA: Daniela! *(To ENZO.)* You are playing with very dangerous things, Enzo. You must stick to making the stained glass for the cathedral. That is God's work. This other is...

ENZO: Is man's work. God gave us strong minds so we can do greater things. Perhaps glass such as this can be used to do great things!

GABRIELLA: Tricks of the eye! Deception! Perhaps evil things!

ENZO: I use metal tools because God did not give me hands hard enough to cut glass! The men who make the stained glass add powders and bits of iron when they make the glass because God did not give them colored glass! In fact, God did not give man glass at all! It had to be made by man!

GABRIELLA: You are just trying to confuse me with your fancy words!

DANIELA: *(ENTERS helping NONNA walk unsteadily with a walking stick.)* This way, Nonna...

NONNA: What is all the excitement, my child?

GABRIELLA: Nonna! Daniela, what is the meaning of this? Your grandma was resting in the kitchen!

DANIELA: I have to show her something!

NONNA: Little Daniela was so excited, I had to come! *(Squints and looks around.)* But where are we, little one?

ENZO: This is my workshop, Nonna.

NONNA: Your workshop, Enzo? But I haven't been in here in years!

GABRIELLA: Because it is too dangerous! *(Goes to her.)* Let us go back to the kitchen—

DANIELA: But first I have to show her something, Mamma!

NONNA: *(Goes to the table.)* Enzo, another panel for the cathedral?

ENZO: Yes, Nonna.

NONNA: *(Squints and leans over the table.)* Is it St. Anthony?

DANIELA: It is St. Cecilia, Nonna! *(Picks up the piece of curved glass.)*

GABRIELLA: You know your Grandma cannot see well, Daniela. Take her back to the kitchen—

DANIELA: Now look at it through this, Nonna. *(Holds the glass before NONNA'S eyes.)*

NONNA: Ah! It is St. Cecilia! Now I see her!

DANIELA: *(Brings NONNA close to GABRIELLA.)* And look at this, Nonna! *(Holds the glass in front of GABRIELLA'S necklace.)* Look at Mamma's crucifix!

NONNA: Oh! I see it! It is the one I gave you, Gabriella, when you were little.

GABRIELLA: I wear it every day, Nonna.

NONNA: I have not seen it in years. May I hold that miracle thing, Daniela?

DANIELA: Here, Nonna! *(Gives her the glass.)*

NONNA: Why... it is just a piece of glass!

ENZO: A special piece of glass, Nonna.

NONNA: Has it been blessed by God?

ENZO: In a way, it has. But made by me. It is curved in such a way that it helps the eye to better see.

NONNA: Even my old eyes?

DANIELA: Yes! Nonna, you can look at all kinds of things!

NONNA: *(Looks at DANIELA through the glass and moves closer to her face.)* My, Daniela, how you have grown! And such a pretty young girl you are! Oh, you will have beautiful babies someday!

ENZO: Didn't I say so, little one? *(LIGHTS FADE to BLACK.)*

AFTERMATH

Although there is some evidence the Greeks and Romans used shaped glass to magnify images, the earliest use of eyeglasses is not found until the late thirteenth century in Northern Italy. They are mentioned in letters by 1301 and first show up in Italian paintings in 1352. The lenses were framed and held together by a rivet which allowed them to be adjustable and attach to the nose. By 1727, eyeglasses had frames that rested on the nose and the ears. A few decades later, Benjamin Franklin invented bifocals. Although the concept of contact lenses goes all the way back to Leonardo da Vinci, the first practical pair of glass lenses that sit on the surface of the eye were not made until 1888. The modern kind of small contact lenses, which are placed on the cornea of the eye, were first available in 1949. Today, most glasses and contact lenses are made of plastic rather than glass, but the basic principles of the lens remain.

MIRROR IMAGE SCRIBBLING
(1519)

BACKGROUND

The final three years in the life of the artist, inventor, and anatomist, Leonardo da Vinci (1452-1519), were spent in France, where his patron, King Francis I, set Leonardo up with lodgings and a workspace in the manor house Clos Lucé near the royal Château d'Amboise. The young Italian artist Count Francesco Melzi was Leonardo's most faithful pupil, remaining with the bedridden Leonardo until he died of a stroke at the age of 67. Much of Leonardo's money, art, scientific notebooks, and sketches were left to Melzi. The French king gave Leonardo a lavish funeral and had the artist buried in the Church of Saint-Florentin at the Château d'Amboise in May of 1519.

CHARACTERS

COUNT FRANCESCO
    MELZI (M) .... Italian artist
VICOMTE DE
    GOULAINE* (M) .... advisor to King Frances I of France

*Fictional character

SETTING

Time: A September morning in 1519.

Place: Leonardo da Vinci's workroom in Clos Lucé near the Château d'Amboise, France.

SET DESCRIPTION

The workroom consists of three tables piled with flat and rolled papers, bound books, and a few wooden models. There is a hand mirror on one of the tables. There are also three stools and boxes filled with models. At one end of the room is a fireplace, and next to it is a large valise.

LIGHTS UP on the late Leonardo da Vinci's workroom. GOULAINE is at one of the tables, going through the drawings, looking at each one, and separating them into two piles. After a few moments, COUNT FRANCESCO MELZI ENTERS. Surprised to see GOULAINE, he stops in his tracks.

MELZI: Vicomte de Goulaine! What... what are you doing here?

GOULAINE: *(Doesn't stop to look at MELZI.)* One might ask the same of you, Count Francesco Melzi.

MELZI: I come every day. I am working on organizing Master Leonardo's papers, his sketches and notebooks, and—

GOULAINE: I am here by orders of the King of France. I think my reason is better than yours.

MELZI: May I ask for what purpose His Highness sent you here?

GOULAINE: Oh, nothing specific. Just to see how you are getting on.

MELZI: I am surprised the king did not inquire directly. Or come himself. He often came to these rooms when Master Leonardo was alive.

GOULAINE: Really, my young count, even an artist's assistant must realize the King of France has more important things to do than go through a lot of papers which do not even belong to him. Leonardo left all this to you, I understand.

MELZI: You know very well he did, Vicomte de Goulaine.

GOULAINE: All the same, King Francis was very fond of Leonardo and is interested in what will become of his work. As the king's advisor in... many matters, I was entrusted to represent his interests in the late Leonardo.

MELZI: Perhaps I can satisfy your curiosity, Vicomte de Goulaine. You know where all the paintings have gone.

GOULAINE: Such a pity there were not more. About a dozen, I hear. The king ended up with only that insignificant little portrait called Mona Lisa.

MELZI: Master Leonardo abandoned painting many years ago, but there are hundreds of sketches—beautiful drawings and sketches. And then he turned his attention to more scientific studies.

GOULAINE: Yes, another pity. For such a fine artist to waste his time in all those anatomical drawings! I see dozens of them here. Quite disgusting, in my opinion.

MELZI: They were studies of the figure and to teach his pupils about the muscular composition of the human body. Of animals, as well.

GOULAINE: And these horrid sketches of dissected humans and animals! They are fit only for the eyes of physicians, if indeed for them.

MELZI: Many physicians have found them useful, comte.

GOULAINE: I believe I speak for the king when I say that Leonardo was an artist extraordinaire and will be remembered always as an artist. All of this other... scribbling just distracts from his genius.

MELZI: I would hardly describe any of Master Leonardo's works as scribbling—

GOULAINE: Honestly, does one want to see the construction drawings of a great basilica or the completed structure in all its glory?

MELZI: Both, Master Leonardo believed.

GOULAINE: And these mechanical sketches. Fantastical ideas that are ridiculous if not downright laughable.

MELZI: Such as...?

GOULAINE: This man has wings attached to his shoulders, but he doesn't look like an angel to me.

MELZI: That is a flying device. The wings are strapped to the body, and these handles here control the motion of the wings.

GOULAINE: *(Warns.)* Count, do not toy with me.

MELZI: I am quite serious. So was Master Leonardo.

GOULAINE: Does such a contraption actually exist?

MELZI: Only as a model. Master Leonardo was still working on the problem of what materials would be light enough yet strong enough.

GOULAINE: *(Picks up another drawing.)* And this? The man hanging by what looks like a giant corkscrew?

MELZI: Another flying device. The spiral turns, thus creating an upward draft.

GOULAINE: *(Points to another.)* And this one? The man is suspended by a large... bedsheet in the wind.

MELZI: Master Leonardo called it a parachute. The air is captured in the cloth and resists the pull of gravity.

GOULAINE: Insanity! I'm afraid your master was obsessed with becoming a bird!

MELZI: The concept of flight was only one of Master Leonardo's interests. *(Pulls out a stack of papers.)* These, for example, are all military mechanisms.

GOULAINE: That sounds more practical. *(Looks at one.)* Is this some kind of wagon?

MELZI: It is a vehicle made of iron that can advance regardless of arrows or cannon shot. It is propelled by a gear mechanism inside.

GOULAINE: Preposterous! And this?

MELZI: A cannon that is operated by steam.

GOULAINE: Laughable! And what kind of armor is this man wearing?

MELZI: There is no man inside. It is a mechanical knight.

GOULAINE: I cannot believe I am hearing this! *(Turns to another pile.)* What are these?

MELZI: Master Leonardo's engineering plans. They are all quite ingenious.

GOULAINE: *(Scoffs.)* I'm sure they are. Why is this bridge upside down? *(Turns the paper around.)*

MELZI: You were looking at it correctly, comte. *(Turns the paper back.)* It is a special kind of bridge that is supported from above rather than from below. It is held up by ropes from these towers so that it can span long distances.

GOULAINE: *(Mocks.)* Across the Adriatic Sea, I suppose?

MELZI: Actually, it was designed to cross the Bosporus in Constantinople.

GOULAINE: *(Shrugs.)* Why not? *(Points.)* What city is this? I don't recognize it.

MELZI: It is Florence. Master Leonardo had planned a way to divert the River Arno and create a series of canals which are controlled by pumps so that the water levels are coordinated with the spring flood season.

GOULAINE: Just what Italy needs, another Venice. *(Looks at another.)* What are these?

MELZI: That is a proposed city in which the surrounding walls are movable in order to better protect the inhabitants from attack or siege.

GOULAINE: Moving city walls! Enough! Had these drawings been made public during Leonardo's lifetime, I fear your master would have ended up in an insane asylum!

MELZI: Vicomte de Goulaine, these are the workings of a great mind! He did the mathematical calculations! He made models! He experimented with each of them—!

GOULAINE: And I'll wager not one of them worked.

MELZI: In time, some of them may have become reality. They needed further study and experimentation. That is how a great mind works!

GOULAINE: Indeed. *(Moves to another table and picks up a pile of bound pages.)* Now this manuscript is interesting. It seems to be written in some kind of code.

MELZI: It's not meant to be code. Master Leonardo was left-handed and wrote in a form of mirror-image cursive so as not to smear the ink. *(Picks up a hand mirror from the other table.)* Look at it through this. *(Hands the mirror to him.)*

GOULAINE: *(Looks at the paper through the mirror.)* Ah... I see. How ingenious. And how infuriating. It seems to be a kind of treatise on art.

MELZI: It is. Master Leonardo called it the Codex Urbanus. It is a collection of his lectures on art— everything from basic composition to the finer element of the mixing of oils. It is very long and very detailed and includes much of his own shorthand or abbreviations. It will take years to decipher, but I hope to organize it into a treatise, as you call it, which will eventually be published in several volumes. It will be the most comprehensive textbook on art that has ever been written.

GOULAINE: That sort of thing will please the king greatly. You must be sure to dedicate the work to him.

MELZI: Yes, comte.

GOULAINE: *(Picks up a notebook.)* And this notebook of sketches includes some superb work.

MELZI: They are studies for paintings and sculptures that were never begun.

GOULAINE: They are very beautiful. The king will be very happy to see them published as well.

MELZI: And dedicated to him?

GOULAINE: If you would be so kind. Count, how are we sure which of these drawings are by Leonardo and which are by his pupils?

MELZI: The work of Master Leonardo's pupils all remained in Milan when he came to France. I was his only pupil here.

GOULAINE: *(Suspicious.)* I see…

MELZI: It is quite easy for me to distinguish between my work and Master Leonardo's work. There is no question in my mind.

GOULAINE: You can tell the difference. But could someone else, say… an art expert be able to differentiate between the two?

MELZI: Vicomte de Goulaine, if you are implying that I would try to pass my drawings off as one of Master Leonardo's, I can assure you it would not take an art expert to see the difference.

GOULAINE: Yet you are a painter, Count. And you paint very much in the style of Leonardo, do you not?

MELZI: *(Seethes.)* I paint in the style of the Italian school. So do dozens of others. None of us can approach the superb quality of Master Leonardo.

GOULAINE: How modest of you, Count. I have seen enough. Good day.

MELZI: What will you tell the king?

GOULAINE: Oh… that you are getting on. He will be pleased to know Leonardo left so many beautiful drawings. And I will tell him that you are dedicating Leonardo's treatise on art to His Majesty. He will be very happy. He so admired Leonardo. *(Points to the drawings viewed earlier.)* As far as these foolish diversions of your master, I will say nothing of them to the king. It would upset him to know that the greatest artist of our time had such an eccentric and embarrassing weakness for the bizarre.

MELZI: But King Francis was always interested in all of Master Leonardo's projects.

GOULAINE: I am sure His Highness was humoring the old man.

MELZI: I do not believe so.

GOULAINE: I fear your opinion is of little consequence when we are talking about the legacy of a great man. *(Goes to the table and gathers up three piles of drawings into one large pile.)* You have a tremendous task facing you, Count. All of the drawings and writing about art must be organized and catalogued and eventually published. It is your job to see that Leonardo's genius lives on forever. And it begins with all this… *(Picks up the large pile.)* …going into the fireplace. *(Drops the pile back on the table.)* Good day to you, my young count. *(EXITS. MELZI takes a minute to get ahold of himself, then picks up the pile of papers that GOULAINE held and gathers them in his arms like a baby. He slowly walks over to the fireplace and stares at it for a few moments, then quickly goes to the valise and stuffs all the papers into it. He closes the bulging, heavy valise, brings it to the table, and sets it down.)*

MELZI: Foolish diversions indeed! *(Grabs the valise and rushes OFF. LIGHTS FADE to BLACK.)*

AFTERMATH

Count Francesco Melzi (1491-1570) was able to save and preserve Leonardo da Vinci's drawings as well as his non-artistic sketches. Today, many of the plans have been turned into models and are on display at the Leonardo Museum in Vinci, Italy. Melzi spent the rest of his life deciphering Leonardo's writings on art, but they were not published until 1651 as *A Treatise on Painting*, nearly one hundred years after Melzi's death.

During the French Revolution of 1789, the church of Saint Florentin at the Château d'Amboise was destroyed, and Leonardo's remains were scattered. In 1863, an excavation of the church uncovered some bone and teeth fragments believed to be those of Leonardo. They are now buried in the Chapel of Saint Hubert at the same château.

THE MAD PROPHET OF MEDICINE
(1529)

BACKGROUND

Paracelsus (1493-1541) was a Swiss-born physician who was a forerunner in the science of toxicology, the study of the detrimental effect of various substances on a living organism. He was born Theophrastus Philippus Aureolus Bombastus von Hohenheim, the son of a physician and scientist, and studied medicine at the universities of Basel (Switzerland) and Ferrera (Italy) before becoming a military surgeon. Taking the name Paracelsus, he soon developed a reputation for being radical in his medical ideas and critical of the current practices by physicians. As he traveled about Europe, Paracelsus was labeled a quack by some, a brilliant far-sighted scientist by others. He published several works on toxicology, chemistry, herbal medicine, the diagnosis of disease, mental illness, alchemy, and the philosophy of healing, many of which were criticized and even burnt in public during his lifetime. By 1527, no medical institution or university would hire Paracelsus, so he became an itinerant healer who barely made a living practicing medicine.

CHARACTERS

WIDOW KLAAR* (F) ....middle-class woman in her thirties
RICA* (F) ....widow's ill ten-year-old daughter
ADELA* (F) ....widow's sister
DR. DIETRICH* (M).................mature local physician
PARACELSUS (M) ....radical younger physician

*Fictional characters

SETTING

Time: A hot July day in 1529.

Place: Rica's bedroom in Nuremberg, Germany.

SET DESCRIPTION

The bedroom is an upstairs room in a city dwelling. It has a door, a small fireplace, a child's bed with a pillow and three blankets, a small bedside table with an oil lamp, a chair, and a chest of drawers.

PROPERTIES

Damp cloth, spoon (WIDOW); coins (PARACELSUS); bucket of water, pitcher of water (ADELA).

LIGHTS UP on Rica's bedroom. RICA is in bed covered with three blankets. Her face is blotched with red marks, and she sweats profusely. The WIDOW KLAAR sits next to her in the chair and wipes RICA'S forehead with a damp cloth. DR. DIETRICH stands at the end of the bed. RICA is only half-conscious, at times moaning but never saying distinct words.

WIDOW: She is sweating so much, Doctor. Please, can I remove some of the blankets?

DR. DIETRICH: Absolutely not, Widow Klaar. She must continue to sweat. It is the evil humours leaving her body. It is a good sign. Have you no more wood for the fire?

WIDOW: More wood? But, Dr. Dietrich—

DR. DIETRICH: We must get this room as hot as possible.

WIDOW: *(Shakes her head.)* My poor Rica...

DR. DIETRICH: We will save your little Rica, but we must have more heat.

WIDOW: I will have my sister bring some wood up from the kitchen when she returns.

DR. DIETRICH: You sister is taking a great deal of time getting those leeches. I told her specifically which apothecary shop to go to.

WIDOW: Are the leeches truly necessary, Doctor?

DR. DIETRICH: I have already explained to you, Widow Klaar. We must get all the evil humours out of your daughter's body before they destroy her. I have determined that little Rica has an excess of three of the bodily humours. The bloodletting removed the bad blood humours. The sweating will remove the choleric humours. The leeches will remove the phlegmatic humours.

WIDOW: But, Doctor, she seems to get no better. Her forehead is burning! And the spots get more and more red!

DR. DIETRICH: Do not think that these humours leave the body without a fight. But we will persevere.

WIDOW: I only hope she can survive the cure.

DR. DIETRICH: I do not expect an uneducated woman to understand all this. You must trust me, Widow Klaar.

WIDOW: Yes, Doctor. *(NOISE from OFFSTAGE.)* I think that is my sister now. *(Goes to the door, opens it, and calls OFF.)* Adela?

PARACELSUS: *(From OFFSTAGE.)* I hope we are not too late!

DR. DIETRICH: That is not your sister!

WIDOW: Adela?

ADELA: *(ENTERS.)* Here I am, sister. I am sorry I was so long—

DR. DIETRICH: Where are the leeches?

PARACELSUS: *(ENTERS loudly behind her.)* I dumped them in the river where they belong! Let them feed off the fish instead of the sick!

DR. DIETRICH: Who is this man?

PARACELSUS: It's as hot as Hades in here! Is the house on fire? Should I call the fire brigade?

WIDOW: Adela, what is going on here?

PARACELSUS: *(Crosses to the fireplace.)* What is this fire doing roaring here on the hottest day in July? *(Takes the poker and scatters the ashes.)* Is this a sick room or an oven?

DR. DIETRICH: I insist on knowing who this... man is!

ADELA: It's a long story, Doctor—

PARACELSUS: Oh, you are the physician! Well, I will make the story short and simple so even you can understand it. I was in the apothecary's pointing out to the fool which of his medicinal wares were deadly to the human body—

ADELA: He was throwing things out onto the street!

PARACELSUS: Not the street. The gutter. And as I was reasoning with the man, in comes this sweet young lady with a bucket asking to buy leeches. "Whatever for?" I asked. "For my sick niece," she said.

ADELA: He offered to pay for them, sister!

PARACELSUS: Indeed, I did. And as soon as we left the shop, I disposed of the leeches on the Maxbrücke Bridge. Oh, I owe you money for the bucket. Here are six marks. *(Gives her some coins.)*

DR. DIETRICH: This woman was acting under doctor's orders!

PARACELSUS: I didn't think she was going fishing with them. "Take me to this sick niece of yours," I insisted. "She is obviously in great danger if leeches are on the menu."

DR. DIETRICH: I'll have you know that I am the little girl's physician and am in total control of the situation!

PARACELSUS: Let me guess, Doctor... So far, you've bled her, you are currently roasting her alive to get her to sweat, and

The Mad Prophet of Medicine

you want to apply leeches to drain what life is left in her. I'm amazed she isn't dead already!

DR. DIETRICH: *(Explodes.)* Who are you?

PARACELSUS: I apologize for not introducing myself. I am Paracelsus.

DR. DIETRICH: Paracelsus! *(To ADELA.)* I send you out for leeches, and you come back with the devil himself!

PARACELSUS: Ah, I see my reputation precedes me. Only three days in Nuremberg and my presence is already acknowledged. Quite satisfying.

DR. DIETRICH: *(To WIDOW.)* I must warn you, Widow Klaar, that this man is a notorious charlatan and a dangerous quack known throughout the German states, if not the entire continent!

WIDOW: Oh, dear!

PARACELSUS: You flatter me, Doctor. Without knowing your name, Herr Physician, I estimate that you have killed more patients with your bloodletting and sweating and leeches than the Black Plague!

DR. DIETRICH: I will not be insulted in this manner by such a person. Leave this house immediately!

PARACELSUS: I suggest it will be healthiest for this poor sick girl if you leave, Doctor. You must have plenty of other patients who are hungering for your expertise, God help them.

DR. DIETRICH: Widow Klaar—!

ADELA: Sister, I believe in this Dr. Para...

PARACELSUS: Paracelsus.

ADELA: Paracelsus. All the way here, he explained to me what was wrong with little Rica, and he made ever so much sense!

DR. DIETRICH: Without even seeing the child?

PARACELSUS: The young lady's description was very thorough. She called it the "spots." One does not die of the spots, unless one is under the care of an out-of-date, out-of-his-mind physician!

DR. DIETRICH: I will stand for this no longer. Widow Klaar, either this charlatan goes, or I do. *(Long pause.)*

WIDOW: *(To DR. DIETRICH.)* For five days, you have been treating my poor little Rica, Doctor, and she is not getting any better. Only worse. I think it best if you go.

DR. DIETRICH: And leave your daughter in the hands of this devil?
ADELA: I do not believe he is any kind of a devil.
DR. DIETRICH: No one asked you, young lady!
WIDOW: I think I agree with Adela. Good day, Doctor.
DR. DIETRICH: You, madam, have condemned your daughter to death! *(EXITS.)*
WIDOW: *(Weeps.)* Oh, dear, what if he is right?
ADELA: *(Takes WIDOW in her arms.)* My sister, you have done the right thing.
PARACELSUS: *(Goes to the bed and removes the blankets.)* First, we must get rid of these blankets and put out that fire before the dear girl dehydrates to death. *(To ADELA.)* Fraulein Adela, we need plenty of water. Buckets of it to put out the fire and a pitcher of it for Rica to drink.
ADELA: Yes, Doctor. *(EXITS.)*
PARACELSUS: *(Examines RICA closely.)* Widow Klaar, she is so weak from the bloodletting that you will have to get as much water in her as possible. You must also bathe her arms and legs.
WIDOW: But what about the... humours?
PARACELSUS: Ah, the good doctor preached to you about the four humours, did he?
WIDOW: He explained that—
PARACELSUS: I have news for you, Widow Klaar. The only humours that exist are in the minds of old-fashioned, pigheaded physicians. That theory is not accepted by enlightened scientists, meaning myself and too few others, unfortunately. You see, the old idea is that disease comes from within. The so-called humours get out of balance and the person gets sick. But I believe that people who are born healthy remain healthy unless some outside force enters their body. Sickness comes not from within but from outside.
WIDOW: Then what can a person do to be cured?
PARACELSUS: Most of the time the body fights the outside force. It has the ability to battle the foreign substance and destroy it. But while that is happening, the body is weak. There might be fever or even more serious effects.
WIDOW: Like Rica's red spots?
PARACELSUS: Like Rica's red spots.

ADELA: *(ENTERS with a bucket and a pitcher of water.)* Here's as much water as I can carry!

PARACELSUS: Thank you, Adela! You douse the fire, and Widow Klaar and I will try to get as much water down Rica's throat as possible without making her gag. *(Takes the pitcher from ADELA, who then goes to the fireplace, pours water on the fire, and scatters the coals with a poker.)* We'll use a spoon at first, Widow Klaar.

WIDOW: Let me, Doctor. *(Sits next to the bed and spoons water into RICA'S mouth as PARACELSUS dampens RICA'S arms with a cloth.)* I hear there are several cases of the red spots in the city.

PARACELSUS: Well, as long as Dr. Di...?

ADELA: *(Crosses to the bed.)* Dr. Dietrich.

PARACELSUS: As long as Dr. Dietrich and his kind don't treat them, they'll have a fighting chance.

WIDOW: Do you really think Rica will be all right, Doctor?

ADELA: Will she, Doctor?

PARACELSUS: Let me put it this way, ladies. In experiments I did at the University of Basel, we found that patients with red spots who were treated with herbs and salt baths and plenty of liquids recovered in ten days.

WIDOW: That is wonderful. So, we must—

PARACELSUS: But the patients who were treated with nothing but liquids—

ADELA: Yes?

PARACELSUS: They also recovered in ten days.

ADELA: Amazing!

WIDOW: And what about the patients who were treated by getting rid of the humours?

PARACELSUS: Most of them died.

RICA: *(Struggles to whisper.)* Mama...

WIDOW: My Rica! She spoke!

PARACELSUS: No time for chit-chat now. Keep drinking, little one! *(WIDOW continues to spoon water into RICA'S mouth as LIGHTS FADE to BLACK.)*

AFTERMATH

Paracelsus continued to write and travel, ending up in Salzburg, Austria, where he died in 1541 at the age of 47. Most of his writings were published after his death, and the so-called "mad prophet of medicine" was an inspiration for the German Renaissance in medicine in the 1600s. The Rosicrucians, a group of physicians in Europe, developed Paracelsus's ideas in the identification and treatment of diseases, germ theory, and even chemistry. Some called the Rosicrucians' philosophy "Paracelsianism." Today, Paracelsus is labeled the "father of toxicology" and considered a pioneer in the field of medicine.

AND YET IT MOVES
(1634)

BACKGROUND

Galileo Galilei (1564-1642) was an Italian astronomer and a pioneer in the fields of mathematics and physics. He was born in Pisa into a modest family of musicians and studied and composed music on the lute before becoming interested in science as a student at the Vallombrosa Abbey. After being educated at the University of Pisa, Galileo conducted experiments and made discoveries in gravity, speed and velocity, the pendulum, and the theories of projectile motion and inertia. Using an early version of the refracting telescope, he was able to discover the rings around Saturn, the sunspots on the sun, and the four largest moons of Jupiter. He also invented early versions of the thermometer and the geometric compass. Galileo's theory of heliocentrism (the Earth revolves around the sun) was very controversial and got him into trouble with the Roman Catholic Church and, particularly, Pope Urban VIII. Religious doctrine taught that the Earth was the center of the universe and that the Sun revolved around it. In 1633, Galileo was brought before a Roman Inquisition and, under threat of torture, forced to deny heliocentrism. All of his writings were banned, and he was put under house arrest for the rest of his life.

CHARACTERS

GALILEO GALILEI (M) .... Italian astronomer and physicist
PINA* (F) .... Galileo's housekeeper
MARIA CELESTE (F) .... Galileo's daughter; a nun
VINCENZO (M) .... Galileo's son

*Fictional character

SETTING

Time: A late summer morning in 1634.
Place: A room in Galileo's small villa outside of Florence, Italy.

SET DESCRIPTION

The simple room in the villa consists of a table and three chairs. On the table are many papers, an ink bottle, and a pen. There is also an old chest upstage with a pile of manuscript pages inside.

And Yet It Moves

LIGHTS UP on the simple room in Galileo's villa. GALILEO sits at a table and squints as he writes. He stops to rub his eyes. PINA ENTERS and GALILEO stands.

GALILEO: Are they here?

PINA: They are down at the gate. The guards are questioning them.

GALILEO: A nun and a lute player! What are they afraid of? That they are smuggling in a telescope?

PINA: Oh, Signor Galileo! Your own children! It's disgraceful!

GALILEO: I have suffered greater indignities, Pina. *(Sits and looks over his notes.)* House arrest for the rest of my life. Take my advice, Pina. Never disagree with a pope.

PINA: I'm just an ignorant country woman, signore, and I don't understand what you've done, but to be kept in your own house with guards at the door!

GALILEO: *(Mockingly, as he stands and crosses to PINA.)* Oh, but Pina, I am a very dangerous man!

PINA: You are? I thought you were a gentleman and a scholar!

GALILEO: That right there makes me dangerous in the eyes of the Holy Mother Church.

PINA: *(Makes the sign of the cross.)* Six months I been here cooking and cleaning for you, signore, never suspecting you was such a great sinner!

GALILEO: *(Laughs.)* Your soul is safe here, dear Pina! *(Returns to the table.)* They've put an end to my mischief.

PINA: Thank God for that! But tell me, signore, what terrible thing did you do to make you a prisoner in your own house? Of course, if it is something I can't understand—

GALILEO: Oh, but it is so simple, Pina. *(Stands and leads PINA DOWNSTAGE.)* I will tell you. *(Points.)* You see the sun?

PINA: Every day if it don't rain.

GALILEO: It seems to be moving. Sunrise, high noon, sunset, and all that.

PINA: Of course it does.

GALILEO: Ah, but I said it seems to be moving. I have proven that it is the Earth that is moving. It revolves around the sun, a journey that takes 365 days—one year! Now isn't that a terribly radical idea to put in a book?

PINA: I can't read, so you can put anything you like in a book. And as for what is going around what, does it really matter as long as there is daytime and nighttime and spring and summer and whatnot?

GALILEO: *(Laughs.)* Pina, I wish you were the pope! *(Returns to the table.)*

PINA: Now you're talking heresy!

GALILEO: The Holy Father told me that the Bible says the Earth is the center of all things.

PINA: The Holy Father should know. And what did you say to that, signor?

GALILEO: I said, "Your Holiness, the Bible was written by men of faith, not men of science."

PINA: Did His Holiness like that answer?

GALILEO: Not one bit. He said if I didn't renounce my ideas and stop writing such heresy, I would be tortured until I did.

PINA: Oh, signore!

GALILEO: Alas, I am a coward, Pina. And much too old for torture. So here I am. Alive and silent.

PINA: *(Looks at his papers.)* Yet you keep up with your scribbling all the day long.

GALILEO: Silent for now, but hopefully not forever. My children—

PINA: *(Remembers.)* Your children! I forgot all about them! *(Starts to leave.)* I must go and see if the guards have let your children through the gate yet.

GALILEO: Thank you, Pina. *(PINA EXITS as he gathers up a pile of papers, stacks them together, then writes on the top page as he recites slowly.)* "Discourses... and Mathematical... Demonstrations... Relating to... Two New... Sciences." There! See what you can make of that, Pope Urban the Scoundrel! *(Goes to the chest, opens it, brings out a pile of manuscript papers, and puts them on the desk as MARIA CELESTE and VINCENZO ENTER. MARIA is dressed as a nun, complete with a large wimple.)*

MARIA: Papa! *(Rushes to GALILEO and embraces him.)*

GALILEO: My little Virginia!

MARIA: Still you call me that! After all these years!

GALILEO: Your mother chose the name, God bless her soul!

VINCENZO: Show a little respect, Papa. She is Sister Maria Celeste now.

GALILEO: *(Goes to him.)* And you are still my only son! *(They embrace.)* My Vincenzo! What strings did you have to pull to let you two visit me?

VINCENZO: The Duke of Tuscany is responsible. But the guards say we have only ten minutes.

GALILEO: The duke? My dear Ferdinando! He has never forsaken us!

MARIA: I remember as a little girl I called him Uncle Ferdinando!

GALILEO: If only we had such powerful men in our family. The duke did his best to defend me at the inquisition, but... the Pope is the Pope.

MARIA: Oh, Papa! It breaks my heart to see you a prisoner like this!

GALILEO: Not a prisoner, my dearest. This was once my home, and it is still my home. I just don't get out and about like I used to! *(Laughs.)*

VINCENZO: I have not given up hope, Papa. The Church will come to its senses. Your work will be recognized.

GALILEO: I believe you are correct, my son. But not soon. Not in my lifetime. Perhaps during your lifetime. Or Virginia's.

MARIA: But what good can I do, Papa?

GALILEO: Pray for me, my dear. And for the Church. And for—

VINCENZO: And for an early death of Pope Urban VIII!

MARIA: Vincenzo! One does not pray for such things!

GALILEO: *(Laughs.)* She's right! Unfortunately. *(Sobers.)* No, my son. I was going to say to pray for a time when religion and science need not be enemies.

VINCENZO: That is like praying for the Second Coming!

MARIA: Vincenzo! You are full of mischief today!

VINCENZO: My dear sister, I know how things are. I am in the real world.

MARIA: And I am not?

VINCENZO: To be quite honest, no. You are not.

MARIA: *(Upset.)* Because I live in a convent, I know nothing?

VINCENZO: You are isolated from the real world by thick convent walls and bells and hymns!

GALILEO: *(Smiles.)* Ah, just what every father hopes for when he reaches the age of 70, to hear his children fighting like... children!

MARIA: I am sorry, Papa—

VINCENZO: I didn't mean to—

GALILEO: No, no! Please continue! It warms my heart to hear noise again. Usually it is just me and Pina, and she never raises her voice.

VINCENZO: You must forgive us, Papa. Surely this is not what you hoped for when you heard we were allowed to visit you.

MARIA: We should be comforting you. Instead we—

GALILEO: Oh, I don't want comforting. When I heard you were coming, I was overjoyed. Not only because I have been here almost a year without seeing you two, but for another reason as well.

MARIA: Please tell us, Papa.

VINCENZO: Is there something we can do for you?

GALILEO: There is, my son. *(Goes to table.)* Your sister was correct. One can live isolated behind walls and still be in the real world. I know from experience. *(Holds up a pile of papers.)* This is the real world. *(MARIA and VINCENZO join him at the table.)*

MARIA: What is it, Papa?

VINCENZO: You have been writing!

GALILEO: Yes.

MARIA: But, Papa—!

GALILEO: I know. All of my writings were banned, and I was forbidden to publish any more of my heretical nonsense. Happily, friends have managed to get my work to countries outside of the jurisdiction of the Pope. There is a publisher in Holland who is planning to print my "Discourse on Floating Bodies" and my "History and Demonstration Concerning Sunspots." They will be in Dutch, of course, but they will survive, and when—as you put it, Vincenzo—the Second Coming arrives, they will eventually be available to all scientists seeking the truth.

MARIA: That is wonderful news, Papa! *(Embraces him.)*

VINCENZO: *(Picks up papers.)* But what are these? New writings?

GALILEO: Yes. Two works so inflammatory that they must get out of Italy before they set the Vatican on fire! *(Laughs.)*

VINCENZO: But how have you been able to write? There are guards! What if they catch you?

GALILEO: Oh, I let them see me writing. I tell them I am copying the entire New Testament as penance for my sins. Yesterday, I reported I was nearly finished with the gospel according to John.

MARIA: But if they look—

GALILEO: They look all the time. *(Laughs.)* But the poor fellows cannot read! *(Laughs harder.)*

VINCENZO: *(Reads the cover of one pile of papers.)* "Discourses and Mathematical Demonstrations Relating to Two New Sciences."

GALILEO: That I finished just today, knowing you were coming. *(Takes up the other pile.)* And this is the work that caused all the mischief. *(Hands it to MARIA.)*

MARIA: *(Reads the top sheet.)* "Dialogue Concerning the Two Chief World Systems." Papa, the one about the sun?

GALILEO: Yes. The theory of heliocentrism. But much more than a theory.

VINCENZO: I thought they destroyed all the copies!

GALILEO: I'm sure they missed a few. But I rewrote it all the same. It was even more difficult to write the second time around.

VINCENZO: These must be smuggled out of the country!

MARIA: Can it be done, Papa?

GALILEO: There are several who will be willing to help. The duke, for instance.

VINCENZO: Of course!

GALILEO: The difficulty, I'm afraid, is more immediate.

MARIA: What do you mean, Papa?

GALILEO: How to get them out of this house.

VINCENZO: We will do it! You can count on us!

GALILEO: The guards cannot read but they will be suspicious if my children are seen leaving with two manuscripts. They have been told to be on the watch for just such a thing. And I don't think they will believe you if you say they are copies of the New Testament.

VINCENZO: There must be a way...

GALILEO: For Vincenzo and Virginia Galilei, it will be next to impossible. But for Sister Maria Celeste...

VINCENZO: I don't understand—

MARIA: I do! *(Picks up a manuscript.)* The "Discourse on World Systems" will fit neatly inside my wimple... *(Points to her head veil.)* ...and the "Two New Sciences" can be hidden under my scapular! *(Points to the bib around her neck.)*

GALILEO: I do not think the guards will search a nun.

VINCENZO: Isn't it dangerous? What would be the consequences if she is caught?

MARIA: I won't be caught. And I will be so happy to be able to help you, Papa! *(Embraces GALILEO as PINA ENTERS.)*

PINA: Signore, those guards are getting restless. They say the time is over. Your children must leave.

GALILEO: So soon? Oh, it breaks my heart to have to say farewell!

MARIA: We must not anger the guards, Papa!

VINCENZO: And we leave with a very good purpose. Goodbye, Papa. *(Embraces him.)*

GALILEO: Indeed, you do. I thank you, my children! *(Hands the other manuscript to MARIA.)* The future will thank you for this, dearest Virginia.

MARIA: Goodbye, dear Papa. *(They embrace.)*

GALILEO: Pina, Sister Maria Celeste needs a little help adjusting her habit. Will you assist her?

PINA: Certainly, signor. *(To MARIA.)* Come into the next room, Sister. *(EXITS with MARIA.)*

VINCENZO: We will come again. I will speak to the duke.

GALILEO: Tell Ferdinando that I thank him with all my heart. Goodbye, my son.

VINCENZO: Papa... *(Hesitates, then EXITS. GALILEO goes to the chest and closes the lid. He then kneels DOWNSTAGE and prays.)*

GALILEO: You are correct, all-knowing Holy Father. The Earth is the center of the universe. So has the Bible and Holy Mother Church decreed. And I will obey. *(Rises and smiles.)* And yet it moves. *(LIGHTS FADE to BLACK.)*

AFTERMATH

Galileo Galilei died at the age of 77 in 1642, seven years after his daughter Maria Celeste died suddenly in 1634 and seven years before his son Vincenzo died at the age of 43. The Duke of Tuscany attempted to have Galileo buried in the honored section of the

Basilica of Santa Croce in Florence, but Pope Urban VIII objected, and Galileo was interred in a small room off of a side chapel in the church. Not until 1718 were Galileo's writings allowed to be published in Italy. In 1737, his remains were moved to the sacristy of the basilica, and a monument was erected honoring "the father of modern science," as he was described centuries later by Albert Einstein. Galileo influenced many fields of science and mathematics and was the inspiration for scientists ranging from Sir Isaac Newton to Stephen Hawking.

TO FRAME MY FACE
(1795)

BACKGROUND

Smallpox is a viral disease that was first recorded by the ancient Egyptians. There are various strains of smallpox, some very deadly and others more benign, like chickenpox and other non-fatal ailments. The word "pox" has been used over the centuries to describe pimples or rashes on the skin. Smallpox manifests itself as such lesions on the skin, but also includes fever, internal hemorrhaging, and irreversible damage to the brain and/or heart. Those who survived the disease were sometimes left blind, and nearly all who had smallpox were left with permanent scars or rashes. Different parts of the world have seen smallpox epidemics at different times throughout history. For example, smallpox wiped out one-third of the population of Japan between 735 and 737. Europe saw a major smallpox epidemic in the late 1700s, leading several scientists to try and identify the virus which spread through the air and affected all levels of society.

CHARACTERS*

LYNETTE COTRELLE (F).......singer in the cabaret
MADAME DESTINE (F)..........her older dresser
                              and companion
DR. RAYMOND
    TRUDEL (M)......................French gentleman

*ALL characters are fictional

SETTING

Time: A spring night in 1795.
Place: Onstage and backstage at a cabaret in Paris.

SET DESCRIPTION

The stage is divided into two sections. LEFT is the stage of the Romaine Cabaret in Paris. There are a few footlights and a curtain UPSTAGE. LYNETTE'S dressing room is RIGHT. It is a small and cramped space with a table facing UPSTAGE next to the door leading to the stage, a makeup mirror with a sponge, a chair, costumes hanging on a rack, and a dressing screen. One of the costumes should be a long cloak with a hood.

PROPERTIES

Parasol (LYNETTE); cane (TRUDEL).

SOUND EFFECTS

Audience applause, string accompaniment for Lynette's song.

To Frame My Face

LIGHTS UP LEFT on the stage where LYNETTE strikes a pose. SOUND EFFECT: AUDIENCE APPLAUSE. She wears a colorful, multi-layered dress that goes just below her knees, colorful stockings, and a large hat with feathers. Her face is painted white with bright red lips and two red dots on her cheeks. She carries an open parasol, which she twirls and poses with throughout the song, sometimes hiding behind it and then reappearing again. LYNETTE speak-sings the song, which has little melody and is more a flirtatious monologue set to STRING ACCOMPANIMENT.

LYNETTE: *(Sings.)* Some girls I know insist on curls
And ribbons bright made all of lace,
But I'd rather a parasol
To frame my face.

A little powder on the nose,
They say, is quite the latest style,
But just give me a parasol
To frame my smile.

So, let the rain fall!
No black umbrella will I buy
When I've my pastel parasol
To keep me dry.

I may get wet, but such is life.
I'll pay the price if that's the case.
I'd rather a parasol
To frame my face. *(Strikes a final pose. SOUND EFFECT: AUDIENCE APPLAUSE. LIGHTS DIM LEFT as LIGHTS UP RIGHT on the dressing room, where MADAME DESTINE is hanging costumes on the clothes rack. She is dressed in a dark, floor-length dress, an apron, and a cap. LYNETTE ENTERS the dressing room and hands her hat to DESTINE, who places it on top of the clothes rack.)*

DESTINE: Sounds like a good crowd tonight, Lynette.

LYNETTE: Better than some. Some noisy soldiers at the back.

DESTINE: Did they like the parasol number?

LYNETTE: I suppose so. *(Sits at the makeup table.)* Oh, I am so tired tonight.

DESTINE: Three shows. And three yesterday, too. You need a good night's sleep, Lynette. No wine with gentlemen admirers. Not tonight.

LYNETTE: Gentlemen admirers... At my age, they are getting hard to come by.

DESTINE: Listen to her! You talk like some old lady but haven't even seen your thirtieth birthday yet.

LYNETTE: It's waiting just around the corner.

DESTINE: So is Monsieur Bonaparte. Now get off that chair and get changed. I'm going to get you home and in bed in record time.

LYNETTE: *(Slowly gets out of the chair.)* I can barely stand up.

DESTINE: Do you want to wait to get home to take that makeup off?

LYNETTE: Oh, it's so hot and itchy! I want to take it off here.

DESTINE: Well, alright. But I better get your cloak. Just to be safe. *(RAYMOND ENTERS LEFT in formal wear and KNOCKS at the dressing room door.)* Now who can that be? *(Crosses to door.)* I'll send them away.

LYNETTE: It might be Pepe with my pay.

DESTINE: A day early? I don't think so. *(Opens the door.)* Who is it? What do you want?

RAYMOND: My name is Raymond Trudel. I was hoping I might have a few words with Lynette Cotrelle.

DESTINE: Mademoiselle Cotrelle is very tired. Too tired to be bothered with gentlemen admirers.

RAYMOND: Oh, but I am not a gentleman admirer! I mean, I did so admire her performance tonight, but—

DESTINE: I'll tell her that. Now off you go!

RAYMOND: But she knows me! From the old days!

DESTINE: What old days?

RAYMOND: Back when... when she was not Lynette Cotrelle.

LYNETTE: Who are you?

RAYMOND: *(Pushes past DESTINE.)* I am Raymond Trudel. I was a struggling medical student who was in love with Helene Ste. Marie. One of many, I'm afraid. I didn't stand a chance.

LYNETTE: *(Dismisses.)* Helene Ste. Marie is dead. Go away.

RAYMOND: Exactly what I thought. Dead. Or disappeared. Or married to a count and hidden far away in a chateau. Then tonight, when Lynette Cotrelle appeared on that stage, I knew she was alive and well!

LYNETTE: *(Scorns.)* Yes. Alive and well. *(Gestures sarcastically.)* And this is my chateau.

RAYMOND: *(Goes to her.)* Don't you remember me at all, Helene?

LYNETTE: Don't call me that. *(Looks at him closely.)* What is your name again?

RAYMOND: Raymond Trudel.

LYNETTE: *(Recognizes him.)* Oh! Monsieur le doctore!

RAYMOND: *(Wilts.)* That was me...

LYNETTE: *(Laughs.)* We all called you "monsieur le doctore!"

RAYMOND: Mockingly, as I recall.

LYNETTE: *(Takes his hands in hers.)* Oh, but we meant no harm! *(To DESTINE.)* Leave us alone for a few minutes, Destine. We are old friends!

DESTINE: Remember, it's late and you are tired. Or have you forgotten?

LYNETTE: Just a few moments for two old friends! Go! *(DESTINE EXITS the dressing room, closes the door behind her, and waits on the stage LEFT as LYNETTE turns back to RAYMOND.)* I remember it all now! You were a medical student and someone started calling you "monsieur le doctore," and soon we all did!

RAYMOND: I suppose I was some kind of joke. All of your friends were so wealthy and had titles and came from aristocratic families—

LYNETTE: *(Sobers.)* Fair weather friends, if you must know, my dear. Gone in a flash of lightning.

RAYMOND: What happened? I knew you had several marriage proposals. I was so jealous!

LYNETTE: The hopeful fiancés were the first to flee.

RAYMOND: Why such cruelty? I do not understand it.

LYNETTE: I... got ill. Very ill.

RAYMOND: But you have obviously recovered! You are as beautiful as I remembered, Helene.

LYNETTE: Helene Ste. Marie... was beautiful. But she is dead.

RAYMOND: You keep saying that. I am a doctor now. What was your illness?

LYNETTE: *(Laughs.)* Indeed? You really are monsieur le doctore! Well, I do not care to discuss it, even with a professional. It is my past, and it is mine to hide.

RAYMOND: So, you changed your name and went on the stage.

LYNETTE: Yes. *(Goes to him.)* Was I so very awful?

RAYMOND: You were... tantalizing! You glowed just as I remembered you at parties in the old days.

LYNETTE: Now I do it for money. How shabby, you must be thinking.

RAYMOND: You are an artist!

LYNETTE: *(Embraces him.)* For that, I am forever grateful, Raymond. See, I do remember your real name.

RAYMOND: I loved you then, Helene, and I still do.

LYNETTE: *(Pulls away from him.)* You must get over that foolishness, my dear Raymond. You are in love with a ghost. It was so delightful to see you again, but now you must go.

RAYMOND: Perhaps we can see each other tomorrow or—

LYNETTE: Never, my dear. You must believe me.

RAYMOND: Helene, I am so confused!

LYNETTE: Confusion is so much better than disillusionment. Goodbye, Raymond. *(Goes behind the screen, and after a few seconds, RAYMOND EXITS the dressing room through the door and meets DESTINE LEFT. LIGHTS FADE in the dressing room and RISE DIM LEFT. After a few moments, LYNETTE comes out from behind the screen in a different dress and takes off her makeup.)*

DESTINE: Good night, monsieur. I hope you have not upset Mademoiselle Cotrelle. She needs to sleep tonight.

RAYMOND: I don't know about Helene, but I am certainly upset.

DESTINE: You really shouldn't call her by that name, monsieur.

RAYMOND: She will always be Helene Ste. Marie to me.

DESTINE: That is all very well as long as you remember that it is all in the past.

RAYMOND: You can tell me, madame. What happened to her?

DESTINE: What happened to all of us? Life plays tricks on us, things change, and we are no longer who we were.

RAYMOND: That does not answer my question.

DESTINE: It is the only answer I have. Good evening, monsieur. *(Opens the door and ENTERS the dressing room. RAYMOND hesitates, then EXITS LEFT.)*

LYNETTE: *(Continues removing her makeup with a sponge.)* Is he gone?

DESTINE: Yes. Are you finished?

LYNETTE: Just about. He became a doctor, you know.
DESTINE: All the better he is gone. Let me get your cloak. *(Goes to clothes rack, takes a long cloak with a hood, and brings it to LYNETTE.)*
LYNETTE: Doctors... What good were they for me?
DESTINE: They saved your life. Stand up and put this on. *(LYNETTE stands and DESTINE places the cloak on her and covers her head and face with the hood.)*
LYNETTE: My life... My glamorous life... Let's go. *(EXITS the dressing room and crosses LEFT with DESTINE. Suddenly stops.)* Destine, I forgot my cameo broach. It's on my makeup table. I don't want anyone to steal it.
DESTINE: I'll get it. *(Returns to the dressing room and goes to the table as RAYMOND ENTERS out of the shadows and confronts LYNETTE.)*
RAYMOND: Helene!
LYNETTE: *(Turns her back to him.)* Raymond, go away!
RAYMOND: I cannot lose you again!
DESTINE: *(Returns.)* I thought I told you to leave Mademoiselle Cotrelle alone!
RAYMOND: No more lies! No more deceptions! I insist upon the truth!
LYNETTE: You insist on the truth?
DESTINE: Leave her alone!
LYNETTE: Since you are a doctor, I suppose you must have the truth. *(Turns to him and lowers her hood. Half of her face is covered with a reddish-brown rash that goes from her forehead down to her neck.)* There, Doctor. There's your truth!
RAYMOND: *(Startles, but recovers quickly.)* The smallpox.
LYNETTE: Hundreds died of it. Thousands. I was one of the lucky ones. Look, Doctor, and see how lucky I was!
RAYMOND: Such scarring... is... not uncommon.
LYNETTE: That is a very comforting thought, Doctor. Thank you very much. I dare not show myself in public. When my friends heard, they fled. My family wanted me to go into a convent. Instead, I decided to hide in plain sight. The makeup of the stage would be my disguise, and Helene Ste. Marie became Lynette Cotrelle. Rather ingenious of me, don't you think? Madame Destine was my childhood nurse. She was the

only one who did not desert me. Together we maintain a life of deception, and we do it very well.

RAYMOND: I... I don't know what to say...

LYNETTE: Are you not appalled, monsieur?

RAYMOND: No, mademoiselle. I am a doctor. I have seen many such faces as yours.

LYNETTE: Well, you're never going to see this one again. No one is. *(Replaces the hood and EXITS LEFT with DESTINE close behind as RAYMOND stands, saddened and confused. LIGHTS FADE to BLACK.)*

AFTERMATH

British physician and scientist Edward Jenner (1749-1823) is called the "father of immunology," the science of making a body immune to a disease through vaccination. In fact, Jenner invented the word "vaccination" and "vaccine." The concept of introducing a small sample of a disease into a body in order to build up that body's resistance had existed before Jenner, but it was a dangerous practice, with the virus or bacteria sometimes spreading to others with no resistance. Jenner noticed that the disease cowpox, which affected livestock, was similar in composition to smallpox. He used samples of the less dangerous cowpox in his trial inoculations and in 1796 found success. News of the effectiveness of Jenner's vaccine spread across Europe and eventually to the Americas and around the world. It is estimated that Jenner's vaccine saved more lives than the work of any other single individual. Today, smallpox is almost completely eradicated, the last known natural case on record occurring in 1977.

NOISE
(1833)

BACKGROUND

Samuel Morse (1791-1872) was born in the town of Charlestown, Massachusetts, the son of a strict Calvinist preacher, and was educated in religion and science at Yale University. Although he was not trained in art, Morse supported his wife and children by painting portraits and promoting his Calvinist ideas in paintings in the classical style. His fame as an artist grew, and while studying and painting commissions in Europe, he was admitted to the Royal Academy of Art in London in 1812. During his celebrated art career, Morse painted many famous people, including two presidents, the Marquis de Lafayette, and a group painting of the House of Representatives, as well as portrayals of scenes from antiquity. While returning from one of his trips to Europe in 1832, Morse met the young geologist and scientist Charles Thomas Jackson (1805-1880) on board a ship to America. Jackson was a prodigy who studied medicine and geology at Harvard and traveled the nation and Europe, surveying and mining samples of copper and establishing copper fields for the United States government. Jackson was an erratic and difficult genius who was interested in many areas of science.

CHARACTERS

CHARLES THOMAS
    JACKSON (M).....................scientist and geologist in his late-twenties
LIDIAN JACKSON (F) ....Charles's older sister
SAMUEL MORSE (M) ....famous American painter
BRIDGET* (F)...........................young Irish maid

*Fictional character

SETTING

Time: A Monday afternoon in April 1833.
Place: A sitting room in a townhouse in Boston.

SET DESCRIPTION

The sitting room is furnished in Victorian manner with a sofa, two plush chairs, two simple chairs, and two tables. One table has electro-magnetic materials, wires, and other primitive scientific equipment on it. An oil lamp, a vase with flowers, and a handbell sit on the other table.

PROPERTIES

Large-handled carpetbag with an early version of a telegraph machine inside (SAMUEL).

SOUND EFFECTS

Loud electronic beep, three second sustained beep, three short and one long beep, two short and one long beep, long and short beeps to spell the word "noise" in Morse code.

LIGHTS UP on the sitting room. CHARLES THOMAS JACKSON sits at a table working on magnetic materials. He wears a three-piece suit, but the jacket is on the back of his chair. His sister LIDIAN JACKSON ENTERS, wearing a heavy Victorian dress with plenty of frills.

LIDIAN: Oh, Charles! I was hoping you would hide away all that mechanical apparatus before Mr. Morse arrives! I'll ring for Bridget to take them away! *(Rings handbell.)*

CHARLES: Lidian, you would hide away the tablets of the Ten Commandments if they were cluttering up the sitting room! Mr. Morse will be very interested in what I am working on!

LIDIAN: Nonsense! Why would a famous artist be interested in all these wires and such? He's painted presidents and the Marquis de Lafayette! *(BRIDGET ENTERS wearing a maid's uniform and cap.)*

BRIDGET: Yes, ma'am?

LIDIAN: I want you to collect all of Mr. Jackson's... things on the table and—

CHARLES: You will do no such thing, Bridget. Instead, you are to remain in the front hall and be ready to admit our guest, Mr. Morse. *(To LIDIAN.)* He was mighty interested in my "wires and such," as you put it, when we met last October on the ship. I will not disappoint him.

BRIDGET: *(Hesitates.)* Ma'am?

LIDIAN: *(Gives up.)* Oh, very well. Do as Mr. Jackson says, Bridget.

BRIDGET: Yes, ma'am. *(EXITS.)*

LIDIAN: I hope you can behave yourself while Mr. Morse is here.

CHARLES: *(Sarcastic.)* Behave myself? Behave myself? Whatever can the woman mean?

LIDIAN: You know very well what I mean, Charles. When the Reverend Patterson was here last week—

CHARLES: Oh, the Reverend Patterson be hanged! An awful bore!

LIDIAN: That's exactly what I mean!

CHARLES: I tried to explain to the old fool the importance of copper in the future, and all he could say was he didn't believe copper was ever mentioned in the Bible!

LIDIAN: All I know is you better watch yourself, dear brother. I read that Mr. Morse is a Calvinist, so I suggest you keep the conversation far away from religion.

CHARLES: Religion! Idle talk! We'll talk about art—

LIDIAN: Exactly!

CHARLES: — and electromagnetism. *(Rises and puts on his jacket.)*

LIDIAN: Oh, Charles! You are hopeless! Mr. Morse's letter said he had something he wanted to show you. I hope it's a painting of his. *(BRIDGET ENTERS.)* Yes, Bridget?

BRIDGET: A Mr. Samuel Morse has arrived.

CHARLES: Send him right in!

LIDIAN: Bridget, does Mr. Morse have a large parcel or package with him?

BRIDGET: Well, ma'am, he's carrying an ever-so-large carpetbag.

LIDIAN: *(To CHARLES.)* It must be the painting. *(To BRIDGET.)* Send Mr. Morse in, Bridget.

BRIDGET: Yes, ma'am. *(EXITS.)*

CHARLES: A carpetbag?

LIDIAN: A large one! *(SAMUEL MORSE ENTERS followed by BRIDGET. He wears a light overcoat, a hat, and carries a large carpetbag.)*

CHARLES: *(Crosses to SAMUEL.)* A great pleasure to see you again, Mr. Morse! *(SAMUEL puts down the carpetbag, and they shake hands.)*

SAMUEL: It was so good of you to see me, Jackson, on such short notice.

CHARLES: May I present my sister, Miss Lidian Jackson.

SAMUEL: Pleased to meet you, Miss Jackson.

LIDIAN: Oh, Mr. Morse! Such an honor to have you in our house! Bridget, take the gentleman's hat and coat. *(BRIDGET does so.)*

SAMUEL: Thank you.

LIDIAN: As for your… handbag?

SAMUEL: Oh, that stays with me, thank you. *(BRIDGET EXITS with the hat and coat as SAMUEL crosses to the table with all the wires.)* Ah! This was what I was hoping to see!

LIDIAN: Really?

SAMUEL: *(Examines closely.)* Of course! I see you've made a few modifications, Jackson, since you showed it to me on the ship.

CHARLES: I have.

SAMUEL: Very interesting. You've spaced the magnets differently.

CHARLES: I wanted to see if the magnetic pull was stronger or weaker when the wires had to travel further from one magnet to another.

SAMUEL: And I assume you learned that distance was irrelevant.

CHARLES: *(Thrills.)* Exactly!

SAMUEL: Even when the friction created was variable?

CHARLES: That part still puzzles me...

SAMUEL: I see... *(Notices LIDIAN.)* Oh, I do beg your pardon, Miss Jackson. This must be terribly boring for you.

LIDIAN: Well, no... I mean...

CHARLES: My sister is just dying to know what is in your carpetbag, Mr. Morse.

LIDIAN: So are you, Charles!

SAMUEL: My bag?

LIDIAN: Is it a painting?

SAMUEL: I am so sorry to disappoint you, Miss Jackson. I regret that I do not come to your home as Morse the painter but rather as Morse the scientist.

LIDIAN: Good gracious!

SAMUEL: I have long been interested in science, and when I met your brother on the crossing back to America, he showed me his electromagnet system, and I became very intrigued.

LIDIAN: I do hope you have not given up painting, Mr. Morse. If so, I shall never forgive my brother!

SAMUEL: *(Laughs.)* No, Miss Jackson. I am still painting. Your brother should not be faulted.

CHARLES: If it is not a painting you have brought, what is it, Mr. Morse?

SAMUEL: Something that I have been thinking about and working on since that day we first met on the boat. *(Brings the bag to the table as CHARLES makes room for it by pushing some of his materials aside.)* It is a form of electromagnetism... *(Pulls out wires, two wooden pieces with metal attachments, a device that resembles a battery, etc., and places them on the table.)* I have experimented with the electromagnetic field and reduced the process down to one wire.

CHARLES: One wire?!

SAMUEL: Yes! When the magnetic field is concentrated into a single wire, it is powerful enough that it creates a sound.

CHARLES: Amazing!

SAMUEL: I'll show you. *(Sets up the apparatus and arranges the wire.)* Now, by moving the magnets like so... *(Moves the magnets.)* ...we create the electromagnetic field. And when this metal handle touches the metal base, we get... *(SOUND EFFECT: LOUD ELECTRONIC BEEP.)*

LIDIAN: My goodness, such an awful sound!

SAMUEL: And if I hold the metal handle down longer, I get a longer sound... like this. *(Presses on the metal. SOUND EFFECT: THREE-SECOND SUSTAINED BEEP.)*

LIDIAN: That's even worse!

CHARLES: Magnificent!

LIDIAN: What possible use could such a noisy contraption have, Mr. Morse?

SAMUEL: As a noise maker, Miss Jackson, not much, but if those noises could be sent through a wire to a different place, it could be the beginning of a kind of long-distance communication.

CHARLES: But can the noise be sent through a wire?

SAMUEL: I'll show you. *(Takes one of the wooden pieces with a wire attached and goes across the room to the other table.)* This ought to be far enough for demonstration purposes. Miss Jackson, may I clear this table?

LIDIAN: Well, I... Of course.

CHARLES: *(Goes to table, takes the vase, and hands it to LIDIAN.)* Here, Lidian. You'd trust no one else with your precious vase. *(She takes it.)*

SAMUEL: *(Puts the wooden piece on the table and places the lamp on the floor. He knocks the handbell onto the floor, making it ring.)* Oh, I do beg your pardon. Now on this table is what I call the receiver. The wire connects them over this distance of ten feet. But, in theory, it could be ten yards. Or ten miles. Now, Mr. Jackson, you stay with the receiver and listen to the sound coming from this metal oval. *(Crosses back to the other table.)*

CHARLES: Certainly. *(BRIDGET ENTERS.)*

BRIDGET: Yes, ma'am?

LIDIAN: *(Blusters.)* Oh...!

BRIDGET: You rang?

LIDIAN: Hold these flowers, Bridget. And be careful with the vase!

SAMUEL: Now, I am going to make the same electromagnetic sounds as I did before, but this time, Mr. Jackson, they will be carried by the wire to the receiver, and you should hear them coming from the metal oval.

CHARLES: I understand.

SAMUEL: All right then. *(Presses the metal handle. SOUND EFFECT: THREE SHORT and ONE LONG BEEP. BRIDGET is so surprised that she screams and puts her hands to her ears, letting the vase drop. LIDIAN barely catches it in time.)* Did you hear it, Mr. Jackson?

CHARLES: Quite clearly! Remarkable!

LIDIAN: I think everyone in Boston heard it!

BRIDGET: Oh, I am so sorry, ma'am!

LIDIAN: Not your fault, Bridget. First time I heard that noise, I nearly screamed myself.

CHARLES: Mr. Morse, this is a magnificent achievement! If you can send these sounds through wires—

LIDIAN: So you can make noise in two places at once. I don't see the use of it, Mr. Morse! I think you should concentrate on painting! *(SAMUEL and CHARLES laugh.)*

CHARLES: Really, Lidian! Use your imagination!

SAMUEL: These noises, Miss Jackson, don't just squeak. They can speak! Listen to this. *(Presses the handle. SOUND EFFECT: TWO SHORT AND ONE LONG BEEP.)* What did you hear?

LIDIAN: Noise.

SAMUEL: How many?

LIDIAN: Just noise!

BRIDGET: Three noises! *(To LIDIAN, apologetically.)* Oh, I am sorry, ma'am.

LIDIAN: Really, Bridget!

SAMUEL: You heard three noises, Bridget, but they weren't the same, were they?

BRIDGET: No, sir. Two were sort of... short. And one was long.

SAMUEL: Exactly! Do you know what I call those noises, Bridget? *(She shakes her head.)* Dots and dashes. Two dots and one dash. I've put together a code in which two dots and one dash represent the letter U.

CHARLES: Have you assigned a code for every letter of the alphabet?

SAMUEL: I have. As well as the digits zero to nine. If someone on the receiver knows my code, he could write down the letters as I transmit them through the wire, and I can send a message miles away. And all within a minute or so.

CHARLES: The noises do speak, Lidian!

SAMUEL: I've applied for a patent. I call it the "telegraph."

CHARLES: A telegraph!

LIDIAN: Such a strange word!

SAMUEL: Or as you put it, Miss Jackson... *(Uses telegraph to spell out as he speaks. SOUND EFFECT: LONG AND SHORT BEEPS.)* Dash, dot... dash, dash, dash... dot, dot... dot, dot, dot... dot.

LIDIAN: What did you spell, Mr. Morse?

SAMUEL: Noise. *(LIGHTS FADE to BLACK.)*

AFTERMATH

Samuel Morse's first public demonstration of his telegraph came in Morristown, New Jersey in 1838 when he transmitted messages over a wire running two miles. With federal support, Morse refined his telegraph and, in 1844, made his famous transmutation from Washington, D.C. to Baltimore with the Bible quotation, "What hath God wrought." Today, Morse code is still internationally known and used for simple transmission of messages. Morse worked on other inventions and received many honors throughout his career until his death at the age of 80 in New York City.

Charles Jackson also worked on many various inventions during his troubled life, but fought to get recognition for them. He ended his days in an insane asylum, dying in 1880 at the age of 75.

Lidian married the celebrated poet-essayist Ralph Waldo Emerson in 1835. It was Emerson's second marriage and lasted until his death in 1882. Lidian died ten years later.

WORDS AND WIRES
(1876)

BACKGROUND

Alexander Graham Bell (1847-1922) was an inventor and scientist who spent many years researching ways to communicate with the deaf, though he is most well-known for inventing the telephone. He was born in Scotland and as a boy invented elementary devices such as a corn husker. As his mother gradually grew deaf, Bell became interested in sign language and other forms of visible speech, as well as the mechanics of augmenting sound. After being educated at the University of Edinburgh and University College London, Bell moved with his family to Nova Scotia in Canada in 1870. Two years later, he established the School of Vocal Physiology and Mechanics of Speech in Boston and worked with many deaf students, including Helen Keller. By 1874, Bell moved away from teaching, retaining only two students. With his assistant, the electrical engineer Thomas A. Watson, he devoted more time to the mechanics of sound, inspired by the widespread use of the telegraph machine. In 1875, he and Watson applied for a U.S. patent for an "acoustic telegraphy" machine which transmitted various sounds, but not human speech. In 1982, he became a U.S. citizen.

CHARACTERS

ALEXANDER GRAHAM
    BELL (M) .... Scottish-born American scientist
GEORGIE SANDERS (F) .... Bell's ten-year-old deaf pupil
MABEL HUBBARD (F) .... Bell's nineteen-year-old
                                    deaf pupil
THOMAS A. WATSON (M) ...... Bell's assistant

SETTING

Time: Early afternoon on March 10, 1876.
Place: Two rooms in Bell's Boston home that serve as his laboratory.

SET DESCRIPTION

Two rooms are connected by a door. An office with a desk, three chairs, and a table filled with electronic equipment is RIGHT. An envelope with patent papers sits on the desk. Watson's workroom with two chairs and two larger tables covered with larger electrical equipment is LEFT. Wires run along the floor from the machines in the office to those in the workroom.

SOUND EFFECTS

Static noises.

Words and Wires

LIGHTS UP on the two rooms. THOMAS WATSON is working on one of the machines in his workroom LEFT. ALEXANDER GRAHAM BELL is conducting a lesson with MABEL HUBBARD and GEORGIE SANDERS in the office RIGHT, where ALL are seated, with the two students facing BELL. They each use sign language along with their verbal speech. Because BELL has been working with both students for more than four years, their speech is fairly advanced.

BELL: *(Signs as he speaks.)* Before we finish... today's lesson... I have some news... to tell you both.

GEORGIE: *(Signs as she speaks.)* What kind of... news?

MABEL: *(Signs as she speaks. [NOTE: ALL THREE will continue to sign as they speak throughout the scene.])* Dr. Bell... is it... good... news?

GEORGIE: Please... tell us!

BELL: I think it is... very good news... indeed!

GEORGIE: Please... tell us... quickly!

BELL: *(Laughs.)* Georgie... you are always... the impatient one! *(GEORGIE and MABEL laugh.)*

GEORGIE: *(Signs quickly.)* I am... anxious... because sometimes... you sign too slowly! *(ALL laugh.)*

BELL: I am not... as young... as you... Georgie!

GEORGIE: You are not... old! *(More laughter.)*

MABEL: Maybe Georgie is... a little too... rude!

GEORGIE: What is... rude?

MABEL: *(Spells it out.)* R-U-D-E. Naughty.

GEORGIE: I am not... naughty! *(Pause.)* Not too much... I think.

BELL: No, Georgie... Not too much! I think you are just... like you said... anxious.

GEORGIE: Yes, anxious. So please... tell us what the... good news is.

BELL: Certainly. First, I must teach you... a new word. *(Spells.)* P-A-T-E-N-T. Patent.

GEORGIE/MABEL: *(Speak slowly.)* Pa... tent...

BELL: *(Coaxes.)* Read my lips... patent.

GEORGIE/MABEL: Patent.

BELL: Very good. Do you know what... a patent... is?

GEORGIE: No.

MABEL: I have read... the word... patent... in the newspaper.
BELL: Yes, Mabel?
MABEL: I think... it has something... to do with... intentions.
BELL: *(Spells it out.)* I-N-V-E-N-T-I-O-N-S.
MABEL: Inventions. Like the... telegraph?
GEORGIE: I know the... telegraph!
BELL: Very good. When a person... makes something that... has never been made before... it is an invention.
GEORGIE: Dr. Bell! You have made... the telegraph?
BELL: *(Laughs.)* No, Georgie...
MABEL: Mr. Morse is the... inventor... of the telegraph.
BELL: That is correct, Mabel. And when Mr. Morse... first made the telegraph machine... he received a patent.
GEORGIE: Is it a prize?
BELL: Much better than... a prize. A patent is a paper... from the government... that says a person has invented... something.
GEORGIE: *(Sags.)* Just a paper?
BELL: A very... important piece of paper, Georgie. I will show you. *(Fetches a large envelope.)*
MABEL: Dr. Bell! You have... received one of these... patents?
BELL: *(Opens the envelope.)* Mr. Watson and I have.
GEORGIE: Can I see? *(Rises and goes to BELL.)* Can I see?
BELL: Just as you said, Georgie... just a piece of paper... *(Gives the paper to GEORGIE.)*
MABEL: But a very important... paper.
BELL: Yes, Mabel. This letter... is from the... United States... Patent Office.
GEORGIE: It says "Washington, D.C." here!
BELL: Yes.
MABEL: May I see it... Doctor? *(Rises from her chair.)*
BELL: You certainly may. *(GEORGIE hands the paper to MABEL.)*
GEORGIE: There are... too many words... I do not know. *(Sits.)*
BELL: They are science words. Not many people... know them, Georgie.
MABEL: Doctor, your... invention is about... sounds... using the telegraph.

BELL: You are quite right, Mabel. Mr. Morse's telegraph... sends and records one kind of sound... and it can be long or short... but it is only one kind of sound.

MABEL: But Mr. Morse... turned those sounds... into letters of the... alphabet.

BELL: Indeed, he did. But that is... a code... which needs to be... translated. The patent... that Mr. Watson and I have... is for a machine that makes... different kinds of sounds.

GEORGIE: But are not all sounds the same?

BELL: There are many... types of sound, Georgie. That is what makes... speech possible.

MABEL: This seems like a... very important machine, Dr. Bell.

BELL: We think so. But there is still much... work to be done... to turn those different sounds... into spoken words.

GEORGIE: You can do it, Dr. Bell... I know you can!

BELL: Thank you, Georgie... for your confidence.

GEORGIE: Con-fer-dance...?

MABEL: *(Spells.)* C-O-N-F-I-D-E-N-C-E. Confidence.

GEORGIE: Con-fi-dence.

BELL: It means your... faith in my work, Georgie. And I am... grateful for it. *(Looks at his pocket watch.)* But I am afraid our... time is over... for today.

GEORGIE: I will come... on Thursday.

BELL: That is correct. *(To MABEL.)* And you as well... Mabel?

MABEL: Of course... Doctor.

GEORGIE: Goodbye, Doctor... Goodbye, Mabel! *(Rushes OUT.)*

MABEL: You have done... wonderful things for Miss Georgie, Doctor. I remember when you first took her on... she was so frightened and... and...

BELL: Quiet! *(Both laugh.)*

MABEL: Yes, quiet. To think that she... has been deaf from birth. It was not so... difficult for me. I remember speaking.

BELL: But you were only... five years old... when scarlet fever... destroyed your hearing.

MABEL: As a child... I did a lot of talking! *(Laughs.)*

BELL: And listening too. You remember sounds.

MABEL: I do, Doctor. That is why your... machine is so important! If you can send different sounds through the wires... as it says in this patent... *(Gives him back the paper.)* ...then maybe you can send... spoken words as well.

BELL: That is our hope, Mabel.

MABEL: I believe you will do it, Doctor.

BELL: *(Takes her hands in his. They are no longer signing, and MABEL reads BELL'S lips.)* Thank you, Mabel, for your... *(Searches for the word.)*

MABEL: Confidence?

BELL: *(Smiles.)* Yes, your confidence. It is an inspiration to me. *(They share a moment as they hold hands.)*

MABEL: *(Lets go of his hands to sign.)* Until Thursday...

BELL: *(Signs.)* Until Thursday... *(MABEL EXITS. BELL opens the door to the workroom and goes to WATSON.)*

WATSON: Lessons over for today, Dr. Bell?

BELL: Yes. Have you had any success with controlling the vibration, Mr. Watson?

WATSON: These charts you have made with the phonautograph show a definite link between the sound levels and the vibrations, but whenever I try to transmit the vibrations through the circuits, they get all scrambled. My words turn into just a series of alternating frequencies.

BELL: There is something encouraging in that. Human speech is a series of frequencies. The challenge is to unscramble them.

WATSON: Right now, what we have is a very noisy version of Morse code!

BELL: Well, that will never do. Come into my office, Mr. Watson. I want to show you something.

WATSON: Certainly, Doctor. *(Both cross INTO the office and go to the desk.)*

BELL: I've returned to the idea of using liquid as a stabilizer.

WATSON: Elisha Gray's water transmitter?

BELL: Gray might be right about the liquid possibility, but the diaphragm needs to be stabilized, and I think the answer might lie in those vibration charts.

WATSON: I don't understand the connection, Doctor.

BELL: The electrical resistance in water is much different than in air. Even in a vacuum, which we have also tried. If I send the vibrations to this needle through the water, I think they might be less chaotic.

WATSON: I see.

BELL: Of course, talking to a container of liquid is far from practical for everyday use, but I believe it may be a beginning.

WATSON: If clear signals can be sent by way of water, we can later figure out how to replicate the process using other means of transmission.

BELL: Exactly. Mr. Watson, let me experiment with this needle a bit and you continue to try to regulate that receiving device.

WATSON: Yes, Doctor. *(Returns to the workroom, leaving the connecting door open. While BELL is looking over his notes, WATSON turns on the receiver. BELL rises and goes into the workroom.)*

BELL: If you don't need them right now, I'd like to reference those charts from the phonautograph.

WATSON: *(Goes to the other table.)* Take them, Doctor. *(Hands the papers to BELL.)* I will be busy with this receiver for quite a while.

BELL: Thank you. *(Returns to his desk in the office, leaving the connecting door open. BELL sits and studies the charts. SOUND EFFECT: LOUD STATIC NOISES come from the receiver in the workroom. BELL is annoyed at the sound so he goes to the door and shuts it. STATIC NOISES DIMINISH. BELL returns to the table. WATSON adjusts the receiver and STATIC NOISES DIMINISH MORE. After consulting some charts, BELL works over the container of water. A puzzled look comes over his face.)* Mr. Watson, come here. I want to see you. *(BELL'S words come through the receiver in the other room, and WATSON stands up, astounded. BELL turns and sees that the door is closed so he shouts.)* Mr. Watson! *(WATSON rushes to the door and opens it, breathless.)*

WATSON: Dr. Bell… I heard you!

BELL: I should hope so. I shouted loud enough. Come here and look at—

WATSON: You don't understand, Doctor! I heard you! Through the receiver!

BELL: What did you hear?

WATSON: I heard you say… very clearly… "Mr. Watson, come here. I want to see you."

BELL: *(Stands.)* Through the receiver?!

WATSON: Yes! You could say, clear as a bell.

BELL: Are you sure?

WATSON: Yes! *(Pushes BELL through the door.)* Go! Listen for yourself! *(BELL goes to the receiver in the workroom as WATSON stays in the doorway, dazed.)*

BELL: Mr. Watson, I think you'd best go to the transmitter.

WATSON: What?

BELL: And say something!

WATSON: Oh! *(Rushes to the water container then freezes.)* What should I say? *(WATSON'S words are heard coming from the receiver. BELL is amazed.)*

BELL: Say all the words in the world! *(LIGHTS FADE to BLACK.)*

AFTERMATH

Within a year, Alexander Graham Bell and Thomas A. Watson developed the telephone and were able to demonstrate it by sending voice messages over a distance of four miles. By the end of 1876, Bell was able to send reciprocal messages at the Centennial Exposition in Philadelphia, and two years later, demonstrated the telephone for Queen Victoria by making long-distance calls across Britain. The Bell Telephone Company was formed in 1877, and within ten years, over 100,000 Americans had telephones. Bell married Mabel Hubbard in 1877, and she was his devoted wife and helpmate for the next 45 years. Bell went on to create other inventions, including early versions of the hydrofoil, the metal detector, and heavier-than-air aerial devices. He died in 1922 at the age of 75. Mabel died the following year.

NO WIRES
(1896)

BACKGROUND

Guglielmo Marconi (1874-1937) is considered the "father of radio," but before that his wireless telegraph invention changed the world. He was born in Bologna, Italy, the son of an Italian aristocrat and an Irish mother and grew up in both Italy and Ireland. Marconi was educated by private tutors, and his interest in science impressed the physicist Augusto Righi, who let him attend lectures and lab work at the University of Bologna. Building on the ideas of Heinrich Hertz's electromagnetic radiation and his concept of radio waves, Marconi created the first wireless telegraph when he was only 20 years old, transmitting signals using an oscillator or spark-producing radio transmitter. He was not yet able to send words through the system, but he was able to send Morse code without the use of wires. Unable to get the Italian Ministry of Post and Telegraphs interested in his invention, Marconi was encouraged by Consul Carlo Gardini to go to England, where he was more likely to get government interest and funding for his wireless telegraph invention. In 1896, he and his mother sailed to Dover, England.

CHARACTERS

ANNIE JAMESON
    MARCONI (F) .... Irish mother
GUGLIELMO
    MARCONI (M) .... her son; electrical engineer and inventor
CARMELO FERRERO* (M) .... Italian Ambassador to Great Britain
WILLIAM PREECE (M) .... British civil and electrical engineer

*Fictional character

SETTING

Time: A Thursday afternoon in June 1896.
Place: A conference room in The Admiralty, London.

SET DESCRIPTION

The lavish Victorian style conference room in the government building is furnished with a table and six chairs. There are two side tables—one on each end of the room—with documents piled on them.

PROPERTIES

Large suitcase with a transmitter, copper sheet, induction coil, telegraph key, posts, and receiving apparatus inside (MARCONI); cane, pocket watch (FERRERO); letters (MARCONI, FERRERO); umbrella (PREECE).

SOUND EFFECTS

Electronic short and long beeps.

LIGHTS UP on the conference room. GUGLIELMO MARCONI sits in one of the chairs as his mother, ANNIE, paces the room impatiently. He wears a conservative three-piece suit, and she is dressed in a fine Victorian dress with a cape and hat. MARCONI'S suitcase sits on the table. Both speak perfect English.

ANNIE: This is outrageous! We are their prisoners! This is just like the English!

MARCONI: We are not prisoners, Momma. Does this look like a jail?

ANNIE: Fancy drapery on the windows! Brass candlesticks! Crystal chandelier! They cannot fool me, these British. We are their prisoners!

MARCONI: Please sit, Momma. You are working yourself into a state of hysteria.

ANNIE: *(Still paces.)* We never should have left Italy. I blame Consul Gardini! I wish he were here with us now. I'd give him a piece of my mind!

MARCONI: Signor Gardini did the right thing. *(Pulls letters out of his coat pocket.)* These letters of introduction from Signor Gardini—

ANNIE: Letters of introduction! What good are such letters when we are in jail?

MARCONI: No one in the Italian ministry was interested in my transmitter. Signor Gardini knows the right people in England who can help me.

ANNIE: The right people?! Look around you, Guglielmo! Where are these right people?

MARCONI: *(Rises.)* Someone is coming!

ANNIE: *(Stops pacing.)* Not another policeman!

FERRERO: *(ENTERS. He is dressed in a high-quality suit and carries his hat and a decorative cane.)* Signora Marconi? Signor Marconi?

ANNIE/MARCONI: Si.

FERRERO: *(Bows.)* Carmelo Ferrero, Italian Ambassador to the Court of St. James.

ANNIE: Signor Ferrero! *(Goes to FERRERO.)* Penso che sia scandaloso! Cosa sea succedent qui? [I think it's outrageous! What's going on here?]

FERRERO: You may speak English, signora. I am fluent, and I know that you are Irish-born.

ANNIE: It is scandalous, Signor Ferrero! We have been treated like common criminals! What is going on?

FERRERO: I came as soon as I was informed by the customs officials. It has all been a little mistake—

ANNIE: Little mistake?! The police at customs put us in a special coach on the train and when we arrived in London brought us to this jail!

MARCONI: Please, Momma. Let Signor Ferrero explain. *(To FERRERO.)* Signore?

FERRERO: *(Laughs. To ANNIE.)* Well, first of all, signora, you are in no jail. This is the London Headquarters of The Admiralty!

MARCONI: The Admiralty!

FERRERO: Yes, young man! Exactly where you want to be, if I understand Signor Gardini correctly!

ANNIE: *(Sour.)* Gardini!

MARCONI: I have letters from Signor—!

FERRERO: So have I. He explains everything. William Preece was to meet the Dover train at Waterloo Station but, well, there was a mistake at customs at Dover.

ANNIE: A mistake indeed!

MARCONI: I don't understand...

FERRERO: *(Goes to Marconi's suitcase on table.)* I'm afraid when they opened this suitcase of yours, young man, they thought it was a bomb! *(Laughs.)* And if you were not with your mother, such a fine lady, they were going to arrest you as an anarchist!

ANNIE: My son! An anarchist! Preposterous!

FERRERO: Because of your Italian passports, the police contacted my office, and I recognized the names right away—Guglielmo Marconi and his mother Annie Jameson Marconi. The embassy instructed the police to bring you here immediately upon arrival in London. I am so sorry I was not here to greet you properly. Annoying official business, I'm afraid.

MARCONI: And who is this William Preece who was to meet me?

FERRERO: Ah, he is the gentleman you want to meet, young man! William Preece is the chief electrical engineer of the British Post Office. He is coming here to see your... what do you call it?

MARCONI: Transmitter. A radio transmitter.

FERRERO: Well, Signor Gardini wrote to him all about it, and he is very anxious to see it. *(Looks at his pocket watch.)* He is late, I'm afraid. This new Tower Bridge seems to have caused a lot of havoc with the London traffic.

ANNIE: My son is a genius, Signor Ferrero!

MARCONI: Momma!

ANNIE: I don't pretend to understand all this electrical rigamarole, but everyone at the university—

MARCONI: Momma, I am sure Signor Ferrero knows enough about me from Signor Gardini.

ANNIE: And only 21 years old! What do you say to that?

FERRERO: Quite astonishing! I also am not very knowledgeable about such scientific matters, but the things Signor Gardini says in these letters are remarkable.

ANNIE: And to think that those fools at the Ministry of Something-or-Other in Rome would not pay any attention to Guglielmo's invention!

FERRERO: It will be Italy's loss, signora, I have no doubt of that. When a young Italian with brilliant new ideas has to come to England to get any attention, it is a sad state of affairs.

MARCONI: But, Signor Ferrero, my radio transmitter will not be for England or Italy or any other nation. It will be for all the world!

FERRERO: All the same, it would have been nice to come from Rome.

PREECE: *(ENTERS quickly. For a man in his sixties, he is energetic and enthusiastic. He wears an out-of-date suit and carries an umbrella and hat. PREECE goes directly to MARCONI.)* A thousand apologies, Mr. Marconi! I've kept you waiting a dreadfully long time! You are Marconi, are you not?

MARCONI: Ah... yes!

PREECE: Splendid! *(Shakes his hand vigorously.)* William Preece. At your service! *(Turns to ANNIE.)* And your mother! Mrs. Marconi, it is my pleasure! *(Shakes her hand.)*

ANNIE: Pleased to meet you, I am sure.

PREECE: *(Notices FERRERO.)* Ah, Ferrero! Thank goodness you are here! Our guests have not been totally neglected.

FERRERO: I do my best, Mr. Preece.

PREECE: It's that new-fangled bridge that makes me late! The one that goes up and down like a seesaw!

FERRERO: The Tower Bridge.

PREECE: That's the one. Every time it goes up, buses are stopped all the way to Camden Town! *(To MARCONI.)* That's why I'm so late. Did I remember to apologize to you?

MARCONI: Why... yes!

PREECE: Good. I am sorry. It's worth repeating. *(Goes to the suitcase on the table.)* I hope your transmitter has survived the crossing intact?

MARCONI: I... I believe so.

PREECE: Well, let's take it out and see! *(MARCONI opens the suitcase and removes the various pieces of equipment.)*

FERRERO: Signora, perhaps I can offer you a more comfortable chair over here?

ANNIE: Thank you, Signor Ferrero. *(Goes to the side of the room with FERRERO and they sit.)*

PREECE: *(Excited.)* This must be the induction coil!

MARCONI: Yes.

PREECE: Marvelous!

MARCONI: *(Hangs a sheet of metal from two posts.)* The copper sheet must be suspended like so, otherwise it will pick up vibrations from the ground.

PREECE: I see. Excellent!

MARCONI: Now the receiver must be placed far away from the telegraph key, otherwise there might be some feedback.

PREECE: *(Picks up the box-like receiver.)* How about if I put it way over here... *(Walks to the window.)* ...on the windowsill? Is that far enough?

MARCONI: If we move the rest of the equipment to the far end of this table. *(PREECE places the receiver on the sill, then returns to the table and helps MARCONI move the telegraph key, the induction coil, and the copper sheet to the far end of the table.)*

FERRERO: What is that wire thing on the top there?

MARCONI: A monopole antenna.

PREECE: Isn't it ingenious?

ANNIE: I always think of an insect when Guglielmo refers to his antenna! *(Laughs with FERRERO.)*

MARCONI: The antenna is used to send and receive the radio waves. You see that the receiver has a little one of its own.

PREECE: Like bees sending buzzing signals to each other through the air!

MARCONI: I think we are ready, Mr. Preece. Would you like to turn the coil and get the electric static going?

PREECE: I certainly would! *(Goes to coil and turns a crank.)*

MARCONI: What we are going to do, Signor Ferrero, is transmit a signal from this telegraph key... *(Points.)* ...over to... *(Walks to the window.)* ...this receiver on the windowsill.

FERRERO: But aren't you forgetting something?

PREECE: What is that, Ferrera?

FERRERO: The wires! There aren't any! I've seen telegraph machines, you know, and you need wires to send—

PREECE: That is why this young man is a genius! There are no wires!

FERRERO: No wires?!

MARCONI: I think you have created enough static to spark the keyboard, Mr. Preece. *(Goes to the keyboard.)* I shall now use Mr. Morse's telegraph code to send a message to the receiver. *(To PREECE.)* Ready?

PREECE: Ready!

MARCONI: Here is the message... *(Taps the telegraph keys: dash-dot/dash-dash-dash/dot-dash-dash/dot-dot/dot-dash-dot/dot/dot-dot-dot. SOUND EFFECT: ELECTRONIC DOTS AND DASHES are simultaneously heard coming from the receiver. When MARCONI is finished, PREECE stops cranking and ALL are silent for a moment.)*

ANNIE: What did you spell, Guglielmo?

PREECE: "No wires."

MARCONI: Exactly.

FERRERO: *(Rises.)* This is remarkable! Do you know what it means, Mr. Preece?

PREECE: Messages sent without wires. And not just across a room.

MARCONI: With a better antenna and a more sophisticated induction coil, messages could be sent over great distances!

PREECE: Over water! From land to ships at sea! Or from ship to ship!

FERRERO: Astounding!

ANNIE: I told you my son was a genius!

PREECE: I notice the frequency varies, Mr. Marconi. The fluctuation probably comes from the copper. But I imagine that can be controlled.

MARCONI: Actually, Mr. Preece, that fluctuation may turn out to be the most significant part of the radio transmitter.

PREECE: How so?

MARCONI: Mr. Morse's code signals only need a steady short and long sound on one frequency. But there are many frequencies, high ones and low ones. If they can be utilized, one can send messages that are not just dots and dashes but more complex like—

PREECE: *(Realizes.)* —the human voice.

MARCONI: In theory, yes, the human voice.

FERRERO: And all without wires! *(LIGHTS FADE to BLACK.)*

AFTERMATH

In March 1897, Guglielmo Marconi demonstrated his radio transmitter for the British government by sending signals nearly four miles across Salisbury Plain. Two months later, he sent the first signals over water, a length of ten miles. Marconi's radio transmitter was soon used across Europe and America, and he became famous. By 1902, Marconi was sending messages across the Atlantic Ocean, and the use of the telegraph during the sinking of the Titanic in 1912 made ship-to-ship radio telegraphing essential. Marconi's dream of transmitting the human voice was not perfected until the 1910s, and radio broadcasting as we know it did not come until the 1920s. In Europe, radios were commonly called "Marconi's" for several decades. He died in 1937 at the age of 63.

William Preece, who championed Marconi's work in Great Britain, was also an inventor in the field of railroad signal communication. He was knighted in 1899 and died in 1913 at the age of 79.

THE TRAIN TO TUSKEGEE
(1901)

BACKGROUND

George Washington Carver (1860s-1943) was one of the most prominent and famous Blacks of the first half of the twentieth century because of his work as an agricultural scientist, environmentalist, and inventor. He was born into slavery in rural Missouri on an unknown date in the first half of the 1860s, but at one week old, he and his mother were kidnapped and sold to a slave owner in Kentucky. Their original owner, Moses Carver, found George and brought him back to Missouri where, after slavery was abolished, Moses and his wife raised George and his brother as their own children. George showed remarkable intelligence as a child and, in order to get an education, had to leave his hometown to find a school that would accept a Black student. Denied a college education, Carver set up his own laboratory and started to experiment with plants, at the same time farming seventeen acres with different crops and trees. His discoveries in plant productivity brought him to the attention of Iowa State Agricultural College (today Iowa State University), where he enrolled in 1891 as the first Black student. Carver joined the faculty after finishing his studies there, and his fame reached the attention of the celebrated Black educator Booker T. Washington. It was Washington who hired Carver to teach at the renowned Tuskegee Institute in Alabama, a position Carver held for 47 years. As well as teaching, Carver continued to experiment with ways to improve farming methods and develop uses for lesser-used crops such as the peanut and the sweet potato, earning him the nickname "Peanutman." He also toured extensively and lectured on his methods, spreading his ideas about agricultural improvements.

CHARACTERS

ZEBADIAH
    FERGUSON* (M) .... White farmer
MAVIS FERGUSON* (F) .... his wife
GEORGE WASHINGTON
    CARVER (M) .... Black agricultural scientist

*Fictional characters

SETTING

Time: An early Tuesday morning in 1901.
Place: A train platform at a station in the small, rural town of Plantersville, Alabama.

SET DESCRIPTION

A backdrop of a shed with its only door padlocked shut functions as the train station. There are two benches on the platform, one marked "Whites Only" and the other "Colored."

PROPERTIES

Suitcase, book, pamphlet, hat (GEORGE); suitcase (ZEBADIAH); oversized purse (MAVIS).

SOUND EFFECTS

Approaching steam engine, train coming to a stop, steam engine departing.

The Train to Tuskegee

LIGHTS UP on the train platform. GEORGE WASHINGTON CARVER sits on the "Colored" bench reading a book, his suitcase on the ground next to him. He wears a simple, dark suit, and his hat sits on the bench next to him. ZEBADIAH ENTERS with his wife MAVIS, both dressed in rather threadbare traveling attire. ZEBADIAH carries a beat-up suitcase, and MAVIS carries an oversized purse similar to a carpetbag. They pay no attention to GEORGE as they see the door to the station house is padlocked.

ZEBADIAH: *(Lets the suitcase drop to the platform.)* Just look at that! They ain't even open yet!

MAVIS: Well, we are mighty early, Zebadiah! T'ain't even six o'clock yet.

ZEBADIAH: *(Pounds on the door.)* Ought to be someone here. We got to buy our tickets. Can't get on the train without no tickets.

MAVIS: What time did Myrtle say the train is supposed to come?

ZEBADIAH: Six-thirty or thereabouts.

MAVIS: There. We got plenty of time.

ZEBADIAH: We got to get on that train, Mavis. Ain't another 'til tomorrow. We been gone four days as it is. I'm a-feared of what the farm is turned into with Amos in charge.

MAVIS: Amos means well.

ZEBADIAH: Amos Hardy can't manage a chicken coop, no less an entire farm! *(Bangs on the door again and shouts.)* Is anybody in there?

GEORGE: There's no need to worry, sir. You can get your tickets on the train.

ZEBADIAH: What's that, boy?

GEORGE: They sell tickets on the train. That's how I'm buying my ticket.

MAVIS: You hear that, Zebadiah?

ZEBADIAH: How's come you know that, boy?

GEORGE: I've changed trains here before. This station is hardly ever open.

MAVIS: So we got nothin' to worry about then. *(Crosses to the "Whites Only" bench.)* Come and sit, Zebadiah. *(Sits.)* No need to be standing the whole time we got to wait.

ZEBADIAH: *(Picks up the suitcase, goes to the bench, and sits.)* I hope that colored boy knows what he's talkin' about. *(They make no attempt to lower their voices as they talk about GEORGE as if he wasn't there.)*

MAVIS: He says he's got on the train here before. Besides, look how nice he's dressed. He must know.
ZEBADIAH: Probably just a house servant.
MAVIS: I wonder if he's headin' in our direction?
ZEBADIAH: Ain't no coloreds like that in Baldwin County.
MAVIS: Can't be too many trains stopping here at Plantersville. *(Rises and takes a few steps toward GEORGE.)* Young man, are you taking the 630 south?
ZEBADIAH: Mavis! Sit down and behave yourself!
GEORGE: *(Rises.)* No, ma'am. There's a 605 going east.
MAVIS: Oh. We're going south to Baldwin County. That's where our farm is. We come up to Plantersville for my sister's funeral—
ZEBADIAH: *(Rises.)* Mavis! No reason to go telling everyone our personal business!
GEORGE: I'm awful sorry to hear that, ma'am. I truly am.
MAVIS: Georgette has been sickly for so long. I reckon it was a blessing in a way.
GEORGE: Yes, ma'am. All the same, a sad occasion.
MAVIS: Yes. A sad occasion.
ZEBADIAH: Oh, for God's sake! *(Sits back down.)*
MAVIS: Where you be headin', if you don't mind my askin'?
GEORGE: Not at all, ma'am. Tuskegee.
MAVIS: Oh, we never been there. *(To ZEBADIAH.)* Have we, Zebadiah?
ZEBADIAH: You know durn well we ain't.
MAVIS: *(To GEORGE.)* We hardly been anywhere. They got the institute there, don't they? The one for coloreds?
GEORGE: That's right, ma'am. The Tuskegee Institute.
MAVIS: Are you a student there?
GEORGE: I was, ma'am. Indeed, I was.
ZEBADIAH: What you do now, boy? House servant, I suspect.
GEORGE: No, sir. Now I teach at the institute. *(A long pause as MAVIS and ZEBADIAH are dumbstruck.)* You mentioned before you had a farm?
MAVIS: *(Practically speechless.)* That's right…
GEORGE: May I ask what kind of farm you have?
MAVIS: Cotton, mostly.

GEORGE: I ask because I teach all about different kinds of farming at the institute, including cotton farming.

ZEBADIAH: *(Grumbles.)* Don't have to go to school to know how to plant cotton. My daddy farmed cotton afore me, and I been doin' it for nigh on 20 years! *(Rises.)* I don't suppose you go out in that fancy suit and do any cotton farming, do you, boy?

GEORGE: All the time, sir. Not in these clothes, no sir, but I plant cotton and soybeans and potatoes and all sorts of things. Then I study how they grow, what kind of soil is best for them, and... that sort of thing. I'm only dressed up like this because I'm returning from Russellville where I gave a talk to some folks about farming.

MAVIS: Ain't that something!

ZEBADIAH: What kind of folks? Them that don't know one end of a hoe from another?

GEORGE: *(Hesitates.)* No... Actually, they were cotton farmers.

ZEBADIAH: *(Fumes.)* Are you sassing me, boy?

GEORGE: No, sir. Not one bit. You see, these farmers were having their troubles. It seems every year the cotton crop was getting weaker and weaker. They used to get cotton the size of your fist, but the last few years, they were seeing just scrawny little tuffs of cotton.

MAVIS: Why, that's just what's happening to us!

ZEBADIAH: Mavis, you shut your mouth this instant!

MAVIS: But it's the truth, Zebadiah! *(To GEORGE.)* We're worried sick about it. It seems we can't get a decent cotton crop no more. And it ain't been drought or too much rain or nothin' like that!

ZEBADIAH: Mavis!

MAVIS: It's like we been doin' something wrong, but it's what we always done in the past! *(Starts to cry.)*

ZEBADIAH: *(To GEORGE.)* You pay her no mind, boy! *(Grabs MAVIS and guides her to the bench, where they both sit.)* Now you behave yourself, Mavis! There ain't no reason to be carryin' on like this!

MAVIS: *(Still weeps.)* But I know you are worried sick over this, Zebadiah, even though you won't talk about it! And I feel so hopeless 'cause I can't help you!

ZEBADIAH: You just leave all that to me. You got your hands full with the chickens and the kitchen garden. Just set still and things will work out.

MAVIS: *(Stands, resolute.)* I been setting still for too long, and things ain't working out! *(Goes over to GEORGE.)* Young man, what did you tell them folks? The cotton farmers who can't get a good crop no more?

ZEBADIAH: *(Scoffs.)* That's right! Let's ask the colored boy!

MAVIS: *(To GEORGE.)* Was you able to help them?

GEORGE: It wasn't just me, ma'am. It's what we have discovered at the institute.

MAVIS: What was it you found?

GEORGE: First of all, it's not that you are doing anything wrong in your cotton planting.

ZEBADIAH: I coulda told you that.

GEORGE: It's your soil. After so many years of growing cotton, the soil loses it nitrogen content. Cotton demands a lot of nitrogen, so we recommend crop rotation.

MAVIS: What's that?

GEORGE: For a few years, you plant something other than cotton, something that actually returns nitrogen to the soil.

ZEBADIAH: But we're cotton farmers. Always been!

MAVIS: And it's ruining us!

GEORGE: Sweet potatoes, for example, provide a lot of nitrogen to the soil. So do soybeans, pecans, cowpeas, and peanuts.

ZEBADIAH: Peanuts! The market wants cotton! Not peanuts!

GEORGE: While peanuts by themselves have limited market value—

MAVIS: Folks like peanut butter, I suppose.

ZEBADIAH: *(Scowls.)* Peanut butter!

GEORGE: But at the institute, I have developed many other uses for the peanut. Peanut oil, for example, is cheaper and healthier than conventional cooking oil. And a lotion made from peanuts has proven to be very effective on muscle pain. But whether it's peanuts or some other nitrogen-producing crop, the soil is soon replenished, and after a few years, your cotton crop will be as plentiful as you remember.

MAVIS: Oh, Zebadiah!

ZEBADIAH: It sounds like a lot of hooey to me. You're not some kind of fly-by-night salesman, are you, boy?

GEORGE: *(Smiles.)* No, sir. I'm not selling anything. You will want to learn more about crop rotation before you do anything. *(Takes a pamphlet from his coat pocket.)* Here is a pamphlet I wrote for the institute which explains all about soil depletion and crop rotation. *(Goes to them, holding out the pamphlet.)* It will answer many questions you may have. *(MAVIS and ZEBADIAH are embarrassed and make no attempt to take the pamphlet. A pause.)* It's free.

MAVIS: No, thank you... very kindly.

GEORGE: But...?

ZEBADIAH: We can't read.

GEORGE: Oh. I understand—

MAVIS: *(Grabs the pamphlet.)* But we'll find someone who can read it to us.

ZEBADIAH: *(To MAVIS.)* Who do we know that can read?

MAVIS: Lots of folks. Like... Francine Wiley. She can read... some. *(SOUND EFFECT: STEAM ENGINE APPROACHES.)*

GEORGE: I think you will find it very helpful. Here's my train. *(Picks up his suitcase and his hat.)*

MAVIS: *(Looks at the cover of the pamphlet.)* Young man... you say you wrote this?

GEORGE: That is correct, ma'am.

MAVIS: *(Goes to him with the pamphlet.)* Is your name here on the cover?

GEORGE: It is indeed, ma'am.

MAVIS: Can you show me?

GEORGE: Certainly. *(Points.)* Right here. George Washington Carver. *(SOUND EFFECT: TRAIN COMES TO A STOP.)*

MAVIS: Well ain't that something! It was a pleasure meeting you, Mr. George Washington Carver!

GEORGE: The pleasure was all mine. *(Tips his hat.)* My coach is at the end of the train, so I better scoot if I want to get back there in time. *(To ZEBADIAH.)* Good day to you, sir. And I wish both of you great success with your farm. *(Runs OFF.)*

MAVIS: Goodbye!

ZEBADIAH: *(After a pause.)* Well... I'll be gosh-darned! *(SOUND EFFECT: STEAM ENGINE DEPARTS. MAVIS and ZEBADIAH watch the train leave in awe as LIGHTS FADE to BLACK.)*

AFTERMATH

George Washington Carver's fame grew because of his writings and lectures on improving farming techniques, his development of over one hundred uses for the peanut, and his environmental work, which was well ahead of its time. He was honored by universities, presidents, and international societies. He lobbied successfully for a tariff to be put on cheaply priced peanuts from China in order to protect the American peanut farmers. Carver continued to be a close friend to Booker T. Washington, though they also had their disagreements. When Carver died from complications from a fall down a flight of steps at the age of about 78, he was buried next to Washington at Tuskegee University. Carver's legacy is maintained by the Carver Museum in Tuskegee and the George Washington Carver Foundation.

LITTLE CURIES
(1914)

BACKGROUND

Marie Curie (1867-1934) was born Marie Sklodowska in Warsaw, Poland, the daughter of two teachers who were left financially destitute after the Polish uprising of 1865. Higher education for women being limited in her homeland, Curie worked to save enough money to go to France, where she earned degrees in physics and mathematics at the Sorbonne in Paris. It was there she met and married the young scientist Pierre Curie, the two working on separate experiments in chemistry and physics. When Marie discovered the unique behavior of the element uranium and titled it "radioactivity," Pierre teamed up with her. Together, they discovered the radioactive elements polonium and radium. Pierre Curie died in a carriage accident in 1906 at the age of 46. Marie continued her work, particularly in the field of radiology. When World War I broke out, she championed the use of X-rays to aid in treating wounded soldiers.

CHARACTERS

SERGEANT CORBIN* (M) ......recently promoted young soldier
COLONEL BEDARD* (M) ....mature career military man
MARIE CURIE (F) ....scientist and doctor
IRENE CURIE (F) ....her teenage daughter
                                                    and assistant

*Fictional characters

SETTING

Time: An October morning in 1914.
Place: A field command headquarters near St. Quentin, France.

SET DESCRIPTION

The field command headquarters is housed in a farmhouse requisitioned by the military. The room has a desk with a stack of papers and maps and three chairs. There are also maps on the walls.

PROPERTIES

Documents (MARIE); rifle (SERGEANT).

SOUND EFFECTS

Distant artillery fire, airplanes flying overhead.

LIGHTS UP on the field command headquarters. COLONEL BEDARD stands at the desk looking at maps, wearing full military attire except for a hat. SERGEANT CORBIN ENTERS, wearing full World War I battle gear with a rifle strapped over his shoulder. Throughout the scene, we hear SOUND EFFECTS: DISTANT ARTILLERY FIRE and sporadic AIRPLANES FLYING OVERHEAD.

SERGEANT: Colonel!

COLONEL: *(Without looking up from his maps.)* What is it, Sergeant?

SERGEANT: Two civilians trying to cross the border into the frontier, sir!

COLONEL: *(Looks up.)* Corbin, you are now a sergeant. It is your job to handle these minor nuisances.

SERGEANT: But, sir. These are two women!

COLONEL: Certainly you are qualified to send two females back where they came from.

SERGEANT: But they are in this very odd-looking truck and—

COLONEL: I am sure it has a reverse gear. Tell them to use it and be on their way. The frontier is no place for civilians, male or female.

SERGEANT: Colonel, I tried explaining—

COLONEL: Your job, Sergeant, is not to explain. Get rid of them. I am very busy—

MARIE: *(ENTERS followed by her daughter IRENE. Both wear white medical uniforms, which are mostly covered by long gray capes with hoods.)* Where is that sergeant? We are wasting valuable time! *(Sees SERGEANT.)* There you are!

SERGEANT: *(To COLONEL.)* This is them, Colonel.

MARIE: *(To COLONEL.)* Sir, are you in charge here?

COLONEL: Indeed, I am, madame. I am Colonel Bedard and—

MARIE: I am Madame Curie, and I have permission from General Linard to bring my truck and equipment to the field hospital in St. Quentin.

COLONEL: *(To SERGEANT.)* Sergeant Corbin, why didn't you tell me these women were nurses?

MARIE: We are not nurses, Colonel. I am a doctor, and this is my assistant and X-ray technician, Miss Curie.

SERGEANT: Curie? <u>The</u> Madame Curie?

COLONEL: Sergeant, I will ask the questions here.

SERGEANT: But, Colonel—!
COLONEL: *(To MARIE.)* I don't care if you are Madame Tussaud herself. You can't get to St. Quentin in a truck. It is six miles from here, and there is enemy action on the northern line. You would need a tank, and I don't happen to have one available.
MARIE: Then we must take an alternate route to the field hospital near St. Quentin.
COLONEL: Impossible.
SERGEANT: There is the river road that passes through—
COLONEL: Sergeant, you will remain silent unless you are addressed. Is that clear?
SERGEANT: Yes, sir.
MARIE: But General Linard has—
COLONEL: So, you are friendly with General Linard, are you, madame?
MARIE: The general is the one who has authorized my program.
COLONEL: And what sort of program is that, madame?
MARIE: It is called the Red Cross Radiology Service.
COLONEL: Radio? You send messages by wire? That sort of thing?
MARIE: Not at all, Colonel. Radiology, not radio.
COLONEL: It sounds like much the same thing. *(To IRENE.)* And what do you do, mademoiselle technician? Do you operate the radio message machine?
IRENE: No, Colonel. I operate the X-ray machine.
COLONEL: Ah. *(Pause.)*
MARIE: Colonel, do you know what an X-ray is?
COLONEL: No, madame. And I don't think I am much interested. You see, I happen to have a war on my hands at the moment.
MARIE: I would be very surprised if you did know what an X-ray was, Colonel. Very few people do. It was discovered by Wilhelm Röntgen in 1895—
COLONEL: Röntgen? Sounds German.
MARIE: Yes. But that is not the point. The point is that I must get my truck to that field hospital in order to begin my program for General Linard.
COLONEL: Ah, yes. Your program. The Red Cross Radio...
MARIE: Radiology Service. Yes.

IRENE: *(To MARIE.)* Mother, perhaps if I could explain to the colonel what exactly the X-ray machine does—

COLONEL: The mademoiselle is your daughter, madame?

MARIE: Yes.

COLONEL: So young and yet so intelligent that she can explain to the old colonel something so complex as—

IRENE: It is not so difficult to understand, Colonel! Even you could comprehend it—

MARIE: Irene! *(SERGEANT laughs.)*

COLONEL: What is so funny, Sergeant?

SERGEANT: *(Quickly stops laughing.)* Nothing, Colonel. Nothing at all.

MARIE: Colonel, I must apologize for my daughter—

COLONEL: No need, madame. *(To IRENE.)* Perhaps, mademoiselle, your explanation would be wasted on me. Why don't you tell the sergeant here all about this sunray machine—?

IRENE: X-ray!

COLONEL: —this X-ray machine of yours? If it is not so difficult to understand, it is possible he will comprehend it and tell me all about it.

SERGEANT: But, Colonel...

COLONEL: *(Glares at him.)* What's the matter, Sergeant? *(Pause.)*

SERGEANT: Nothing, sir.

COLONEL: Very well. *(To IRENE.)* Proceed, mademoiselle.

IRENE: Yes. How to begin?

COLONEL: Indeed. How?

IRENE: Sergeant, do you understand what radioactivity is?

SERGEANT: Well...

COLONEL: Answer the young lady, Sergeant.

SERGEANT: *(Hesitates.)* No, Mademoiselle.

MARIE: It is not essential, Sergeant. Do not worry.

COLONEL: Oh, the sergeant is not worried. Are you, Sergeant?

SERGEANT: No, sir...

IRENE: Radioactivity is the result when an element loses energy from its nucleus through radiation. My mother discovered radioactivity several years ago.

COLONEL: Another invention, madame? Next I shall learn you discovered the thermometer.

MARIE: That was another Polish scientist named Fahrenheit.

IRENE: The X-ray machine uses the principle of radiology. It sends radium waves that can penetrate the human body and send back images of what is inside. The waves mostly detect solid objects, such as bones. With an X-ray machine, we can determine if a bone has been broken or if it has punctured a lung. Many other things as well. It allows doctors to see what has occurred inside the body and helps them decide on what action to take.

SERGEANT: It sounds like... a miracle of an invention!

MARIE: That is why it is essential that field hospitals have immediate access to X-ray machines. Not only bones, but bullets and shrapnel also can be detected. A surgeon can determine exactly where a piece of metal has been lodged in the body and attempt to remove it.

IRENE: The difficulty is the size of the X-ray machine. It is very large and heavy, and there are not enough of them to be all the places they are needed.

MARIE: That is the reason for the Red Cross Radiology Service. Each of our specially designed trucks is equipped with an X-ray machine that can move to where it is needed, and right now, our truck is needed in St. Quentin!

SERGEANT: I told you it was an odd-looking truck, Colonel!

MARIE: *(Takes out documents from under her cape.)* Colonel, here are my official instructions from General Linard... *(Hands them to COLONEL.)* ...as well as transit documents and identification papers. *(COLONEL looks though the papers.)*

IRENE: Well, Sergeant? Now do you understand what an X-ray machine does?

SERGEANT: *(Gushes.)* I certainly do, mademoiselle! And you operate this machine?

IRENE: Of course. I grew up in a laboratory where my mother and late father were always working on experiments with radium. Did I tell you my mother discovered radium?

COLONEL: *(Looks at the papers, shocked.)* But... but... you are the Madame Curie! Why didn't you say so? *(Beat.)* Oh, so you did! I didn't catch the name.

SERGEANT: Colonel, we must get them to St. Quentin.

COLONEL: Do you think the river road will be safe enough?

SERGEANT: Quite safe. It is six miles longer but—

MARIE: We must start right away then. Colonel, show me on the map... *(Goes to the desk with COLONEL, and together they study the map.)*

SERGEANT: What you are doing is a remarkable thing... Mademoiselle Curie.

IRENE: It is all because of my mother. She is a remarkable woman.

SERGEANT: If you don't mind my saying so, you seem to be pretty special yourself.

COLONEL: *(Gives MARIE her papers back.)* Here are your documents, madame. There is a check point at Elisé and another when you cross the river at Gallimont. Godspeed to you both.

MARIE: Thank you, Colonel.

COLONEL: *(To IRENE.)* And thank you, mademoiselle, for your very satisfactory explanation of the X-ray machine. Even an old soldier could comprehend you.

IRENE: I meant no offense, Colonel—

COLONEL: None was taken, my dear. Now you two get back to your truck—I say, I don't suppose it is an ordinary truck. It must have a special name.

MARIE: So far we have twelve of them. We hope to have more. General Linard calls them Petites Curies.

COLONEL: *(Laughs.)* Little Curies! Indeed, they are! Farewell!

MARIE: Come, Irene! We must be off! *(EXITS with IRENE.)*

SERGEANT: Amazing women!

COLONEL: *(Laughs.)* Little Curies! *(LIGHTS FADE to BLACK.)*

AFTERMATH

Marie Curie was the first woman to win the Nobel Prize, receiving the award for physics in 1903. She won the Nobel Prize again in 1911 in the field of chemistry. To date, she is the only person to win the Nobel Prize in two different branches of science. She founded the Curie Institute, with a branch in Paris and another in her native Warsaw. Curie continued her scientific studies until her death in 1934 from aplastic anemia, believed to have been contracted from her long-term exposure to radiation.

Irene Joliot-Curie (1897-1956) went on to a renowned career in the sciences herself, winning the Nobel Prize for chemistry in 1935 with her husband Frederic Joliot for their work on the synthesis of new radioactive elements. A professor at the Faculty of Science in Paris for nine years before becoming director of the Radium Institute, her research on the action of neutrons in heavy elements contributed to the discovery of uranium fission. Joliot-Curie died of leukemia at the age of 58.

KING OF THE UNIVERSE
(1925)

BACKGROUND

Cecilia Payne-Gaposchkin (1900-1979) was a British-born American astronomer who is most known for determining that the sun and other stars consisted of hydrogen and helium, which was contrary to the general belief at the time. She was born Cecilia Payne in Wendover, England, and showed superior intelligence as a child, winning scholarships to quality schools. Payne studied physics and chemistry at Cambridge University but was not allowed to receive a degree because she was a woman. After becoming interested in astronomy, she moved to America, where there were slightly more opportunities for women in science. Once there, Payne was awarded a fellowship at Harvard College Observatory, only the second woman to get such a position. The first, Adelaide Ames (1900-1932), was still working at the observatory, which was headed by Dr. Harlow Shapley. In May 1925, Payne was the first woman to receive a PhD in astronomy from Radcliffe College of Harvard University.

CHARACTERS

ADELAIDE AMES (F) ....astronomer
CECILIA PAYNE (F) ....another
HARLOW SHAPLEY (M).........head of the Harvard College Observatory
HENRY NORRIS
    RUSSELL (M).....................Professor of Astronomy at Princeton University

SETTING

Time: An afternoon in late May 1925.
Place: A room at the Harvard College Observatory, Harvard University, Cambridge, Massachusetts.

SET DESCRIPTION

The room serves as a reference and study space for students and consists of two tables, four or more chairs, and two shelves with books and bound manuscripts.

PROPERTIES

Briefcase with a bottle of champagne and two glasses (ADELAIDE); briefcase with a thesis manuscript (CECILIA).

LIGHTS UP on the room at the observatory. ADELAIDE ENTERS cautiously with a briefcase, sees that the room is empty, then calls OFF.

ADELAIDE: It's empty! *(CECILIA ENTERS with a briefcase. She and ADELAIDE set their briefcases on one of the tables.)* I knew no one would be here this late in the afternoon. *(Opens her briefcase.)*

CECILIA: I'm not concerned about any students. I just don't want Dr. Shapley to find us in here… celebrating.

ADELAIDE: Nonsense! *(Pulls a bottle of champagne out of her briefcase.)* If he pops in, we'll just ask him to join us!

CECILIA: You ask him, Adelaide. You've known Dr. Shapley longer than I.

ADELAIDE: Just shy of two years. We're hardly longtime pals. *(Pops open the champagne bottle.)* There!

CECILIA: You always seem so comfortable around him.

ADELAIDE: Working on this catalog together means we spend lots of time together. We even start thinking alike—when it comes to stars. *(Pulls out two ordinary glasses.)* I didn't have any champagne glasses. These will have to do. *(Pours champagne.)* Outside of the observatory, we never see each other. I'll bet he doesn't remember my first name! *(They laugh.)*

CECILIA: Dr. Shapley has been so kind to me. I just wish I was… well, a little less afraid of him.

ADELAIDE: That's just because you're a woman in a man's sacred domain. But you showed them, Miss Cecilia Payne. *(Holds up a glass.)* I offer a toast to the first woman to receive a doctorate from Radcliffe College of Harvard University! Bravo! *(They clink glasses and take a sip.)*

CECILIA: This is good! I've never had champagne before. However did you get it?

ADELAIDE: A bootlegger recommended by the Dean of Women. *(Sips.)*

CECILIA: Back in England, we had wine at Cambridge for special occasions, but never champagne. *(Sips.)* I've never understood America's Prohibition.

ADELAIDE: Cecilia, astrophysics is easier to explain than Prohibition. *(Raises her glass.)* Here's to astrophysics! *(They drink.)*

CECILIA: This catalog of stars that you and Dr. Shapley have been working on, how long do you think it will take to complete it?

ADELAIDE: Well, we are limiting ourselves to galaxies beyond the Thirteenth Magnitude. So far, that's about two thousand eight hundred stars. So, I figure we ought to be finished by... never! *(Both laugh.)*

CECILIA: Now that my thesis is done, I want to concentrate on the stars in the Milky Way.

ADELAIDE: *(Remembers.)* Your thesis! We forgot to toast your thesis. Get it out, and we'll drink to "Stellar Atmospheres"... I forget the rest.

CECILIA: *(Opens her briefcase and takes out a thick manuscript.)* "Stellar Atmospheres: A Contribution to the Observational Study of High Temperature in the Reversing Layers of Stars."

ADELAIDE: That's the one! *(Raises her glass.)* To "Stellar." To Cecilia Payne's thesis! *(They drink.)* Seriously, Cecilia, this is a remarkable piece of work. If you publish that, you'll have astronomers around the world quaking in their boots!

CECILIA: Don't exaggerate, Adelaide. I just conclude that the sun is composed primarily of hydrogen.

ADELAIDE: Dangerous words, my dear Dr. Payne. The current theory argues that the stars are composed much as Earth is. If Earth's crust got hot enough, it is believed it would become another star. *(Picks up the bound thesis.)* But this tiny little treatise proves by the ionization theory that there is more hydrogen—about a million to one—in the stellar absorption lines than on Earth. Therefore, with all the stars composed in a similar fashion, hydrogen becomes the most predominant element in the universe! That's worth another toast! *(Raises her glass.)* To hydrogen! The king of the universe! *(They start to drink when TWO MALE VOICES are heard in the hall outside.)*

CECILIA: Adelaide! The champagne!

ADELAIDE: *(Downs the rest of her glass.)* I'll take the bottle, you hide the glasses! *(Corks the bottle, puts it in her briefcase, and closes it as CECILIA hides the glasses on a shelf behind some papers. DR. HARLOW SHAPLEY and HENRY NORRIS RUSSELL ENTER.)*

HARLOW: Ah! Here you two are! Henry, I'd like to introduce you to the two brightest lady astronomers in America! This is Professor Henry Norris Russell, paying me a visit from Princeton University. *(Takes HENRY to CECILIA.)* The newly graduated Dr. Cecilia Payne...

CECILIA: *(Shakes hands with HENRY.)* An honor to meet you, Professor Russell. I greatly admire your work.

HENRY: Thank you.

HARLOW: *(Leads HENRY to ADELAIDE.)* And this is my invaluable colleague, Miss... *(Can't recall her first name.)* Miss Ames.

ADELAIDE: *(Shakes hands with HENRY.)* I am so glad to finally meet you, Professor.

HENRY: Harlow here tells me you both are making great progress on the catalog.

ADELAIDE: Well, let's just say both of us will be considerably older by the time it is done! *(ALL laugh.)*

HARLOW: Dr. Payne is the first woman to earn a PhD from Radcliffe College at Harvard.

HENRY: Congratulations, Dr. Payne.

CECILIA: Thank you.

ADELAIDE: Her doctoral thesis is a remarkable work!

HARLOW: Yes! About the composition of the sun!

HENRY: I know. I read it.

ADELAIDE: What?!

HARLOW: You read it? How is that possible? It has not been circulated or published—

HENRY: Someone I know, who shall remain nameless, was on the doctoral committee and loaned me his copy. He knew I would be interested in the subject.

HARLOW: Henry, that is hardly academic procedure.

HENRY: It was felt that I should read it before Miss Payne did something foolish.

ADELAIDE: Foolish?

HARLOW: Such as what, Henry?

HENRY: As you said, Harlow, circulate it or publish it.

HARLOW: I don't understand.

CECILIA: Professor Russell obviously did not agree with my findings and does not think the thesis valid.

HENRY: Miss Payne, I—

ADELAIDE: Dr. Payne!

HENRY: Excuse me. Dr. Payne, the work is certainly valid as an intelligent inquiry into an interesting hypothesis, but the conclusion that the composition of the sun is made primarily of hydrogen is, well... suspect.

CECILIA: Is it possible, Professor, that you do not accept the ionization theory which my thesis is based on?

HENRY: That theory—and I remind you it is only a theory—assumes too much. That Indian physicist...

HARLOW: Meghnad Saha.

HENRY: Yes, that's the one. He assumes—

ADELAIDE: She assumes.

HENRY: Pardon?

ADELAIDE: She assumes. Dr. Saha is a woman.

HENRY: Ah, yes. Well, she assumes that stellar absorption lines can be measured by the differing amounts of ionization at different temperatures rather than the presence of the different elements themselves.

HARLOW: Henry, that theory is generally accepted by all astronomers today.

HENRY: Not by me, Harlow. Therefore, I don't agree with Dr. Payne's suggestion that the sun's spectrum can be analyzed by the ionization theory, and that the different elements can be identified in such a way. I still concur with the nineteenth-century physicist Henry Rowland, who wrote that the sun and Earth are composed of the same elements in the same proportions. If this planet were heated to the temperature of the sun, its composition would remain like the sun.

ADELAIDE: *(Impatient.)* I mean no disrespect to the great Henry Rowland, but he made that observation in 1882. Certainly, over the years, better telescopes and measuring instruments have helped us—

HENRY: Would you refute the Law of Gravity because Newton observed it in 1687?

ADELAIDE: I assert that Cecilia—er, Dr. Payne—has just dropped a giant apple on the heads of astronomers everywhere! The current belief that the sun and the Earth are the same has been debunked! And by proving that hydrogen is by far the predominant element in the sun, it is likely that all of the stars in all of the galaxies are also made up mostly of hydrogen! And that is a lot of hydrogen-fueled heat! *(Pause.)*

HARLOW: Speaking of heat, I feel it's getting rather warm in here. Perhaps the professor and I should be moving on. There's so much I want to show him here at the observatory.

ADELAIDE: Cecilia, aren't you going to say anything? *(To OTHERS.)* She's British, you know, and much too polite by halves.

HENRY: Yes, I would like to hear from Dr. Payne.

HARLOW: It is not necessary for you to defend your thesis, Dr. Payne.

CECILIA: Oh, I have no wish to defend it. My theory will be examined and tested by others, I hope, and in time will be accepted as truth. I feel very strongly about that. What I want to ask Professor Russell is why he feels that I should not share my thesis with others?

HENRY: To be quite frank, Dr. Payne, I believe it will harm your career. I read your thesis very carefully, and you are a superior astronomer with a very promising career ahead of you. I would not want you to discredit yourself with this very dubious theory.

ADELAIDE: And what if you are wrong?

HENRY: Then I will be no more than... human. *(Shakes hands with CECILIA.)* It was an honor meeting you, Dr. Payne.

HARLOW: Yes, we must be going—

HENRY: *(Crosses to ADELAIDE and shakes her hand.)* And Miss Ames, I wish you Godspeed on this catalog. I cannot say how grateful the scientific world will be when you and Harlow complete it.

ADELAIDE: Thank you, Professor.

HARLOW: When it is done, much of the credit will go to my colleague Miss... *(Still can't remember her first name.)* Ames.

CECILIA: Adelaide.

HARLOW: To Adelaide Ames.

HENRY: Now, I am anxious to see the new reflector telescope you told me about, Harlow.

HARLOW: Right this way, Henry. *(EXITS with HENRY, and there is a long pause.)*

CECILIA: Thank you for speaking up for me, Adelaide.

ADELAIDE: Thank you for reminding Dr. Shapley of my name. *(Beat.)* He's probably already forgotten it again! *(They laugh.)* Now, pay no attention to what that old windbag said, Cecilia.

CECILIA: That "old windbag" wrote the finest and most accepted textbook of astronomy in use today.

ADELAIDE: Well, textbooks are written to be rewritten.

CECILIA: Henry Norris Russell is also one of the few Americans to be honored by the French Academy of Sciences, the Royal Astronomical Society, and the Royal Society of Edinburgh.

ADELAIDE: Forget his resume! Those folks will be pinning medals on you someday! *(Opens her briefcase.)* I hope that champagne bottle didn't leak all over my papers. *(Pulls out the bottle and holds it up.)* Still plenty left! Where are those glasses?

CECILIA: *(Gets the glasses.)* Right over here.

ADELAIDE: Put them down here. *(CECILIA places them on the table, and ADELAIDE pours.)* What do we toast to next? We drank to your PhD and your thesis and—

CECILIA: And to hydrogen!

ADELAIDE: King of the universe!

CECILIA: How about your catalog?

ADELAIDE: I've got a better one. *(Holds up her glass.)* To Professor Russell and all the fuddy-duddy astronomers who will have to change their minds—and their textbooks—because of you and your discovery, Dr. Payne! Cheers! *(They drink as LIGHTS FADE to BLACK.)*

AFTERMATH

Because both Henry Norris Russell and Harlow Shapley disagreed with her findings, Cecilia Payne downplayed her results as a possible error and did not publish her thesis that revealed stars, including the sun, were composed primarily of hydrogen and helium. Russell proved her theory to be accurate four years later following different methodology and up until recently was generally given credit for this now broadly accepted discovery. The Russian-American astronomer, Otto Struve, later wrote that Payne's doctoral paper was "the most brilliant PhD thesis ever written in astronomy." Over the next five decades, Payne established herself as a groundbreaking astrophysicist, inspiring generations of new astronomers. In 1931, she became an American citizen, and in 1934 she married the Russian-born astrophysicist Sergei Gaposchkin, changing her name to Cecilia Payne-Gaposchkin. She became the first female professor at Harvard's Faculty of Arts and Sciences in 1956 and soon after was appointed chair of the astronomy department, making her the first woman to chair a department at the esteemed university. The asteroid 2039 Payne-Gaposchkin was named in her honor in 1974, and in 1976 the American Astronomical Society awarded her the prestigious Henry Norris Russell Prize. Five years later, she died in Cambridge, Massachusetts, at the age of 79. In October 2000, Harvard University established the Cecilia Payne-Gaposchkin Lecture Series "to honor one of the great scientists of the 20th century."

Adelaide Ames continued to work on the catalog of stars with Harlow Shapley until her untimely death in 1932 at the age of 32 in a boating accident. Later that same year, the catalog covering 1,259 galaxies was published as "A Survey of the External Galaxies Brighter than the Thirteenth Magnitude," which today is known as the Shapley-Ames Catalog.

MOLD JUICE
(1928)

BACKGROUND

Alexander Fleming was born in Scotland in 1881, the son of a farmer, and went on to win a scholarship to attend medical school at St. Mary's Hospital in London. Working as a doctor during World War I, Fleming became interested in bacteria and how infection spread. He became determined to dedicate his life to the study of bacteriology and returned to St. Mary's as a microbiologist. In 1922, he discovered lysozyme, the enzyme in the saliva and mucus of humans and animals that is a crucial part of the immune system. In 1928, Fleming was experimenting with the deadly staphylococci, a germ that spreads influenza and other diseases.

CHARACTERS

ALEXANDER
    FLEMING (M) ....middle-aged scientist
SARAH (F) ....Fleming's wife
MERLIN PRYCE (M).................fellow bacteriologist
MRS. DOWNIE* (F)..................charwoman

*Fictional character

SETTING

Time: Late afternoon on Friday, September 28, 1928.
Place: Alexander Fleming's laboratory in St. Mary's Hospital, London.

SET DESCRIPTION

The laboratory consists of a few tables cluttered with papers, test tubes, two microscopes, piles of Petri dishes, and other scientific paraphernalia of the period. There are also a few stools and two desk lamps. The door to the lab and front windows are indicated OFFSTAGE.

PROPERTIES

Mop, pail of water (DOWNIE).

BEFORE LIGHTS UP. ALEXANDER ENTERS his laboratory, followed by his wife, SARAH. They are dressed in travel clothes which are too heavy for the unseasonably warm September weather.

SARAH: *(Repulsed.)* Ah! The smell in here!

ALEXANDER: It's been closed up for two weeks. What did you expect?

SARAH: Alexander, I don't know how you stand it!

ALEXANDER: Sarah, I told you that you could wait in the taxi. I'll only be a few minutes. *(LIGHTS UP DIM as he puts on one of the desk lamps and begins to check different Petri dishes scattered about.)*

SARAH: I came up because I wanted to be sure you were only a few minutes. Let me pull up some of these shades and get some light in here. *(EXITS and a moment later LIGHTS UP FULL. From OFFSTAGE.)* There. *(RE-ENTERS.)* That's better. Honestly, Alexander, stopping here on the way home from the station! Couldn't it wait until tomorrow?

ALEXANDER: All during our holiday, I kept wondering about something. *(Looks into his microscope.)*

SARAH: Is it always so humid in here?

ALEXANDER: According to the *Times*, London had a heat wave while we were gone.

SARAH: I'm so glad we missed it. Should I open some more windows? Only one is open.

ALEXANDER: We won't be here but a minute.

SARAH: So you said.

ALEXANDER: *(Still looks into the microscope.)* If during the past two weeks something has happened that I was hoping would happen... *(A long pause, then he lifts his head with disappointment.)* No. Not a bit of it.

SARAH: I'm sorry, dear.

ALEXANDER: I was so sure... Well, not sure. Just hopeful.

SARAH: My poor darling...

ALEXANDER: For two years now I have been trying to contain or destroy a certain germ. It grows so quickly, and nothing seems to slow down or stop its growth.

SARAH: Is it this latest influenza?

ALEXANDER: It's that and who knows how many other diseases.

SARAH: You're tired from the train ride from Scotland, dear. Let's go home and you can start fresh tomorrow.

ALEXANDER: Just let me check these other Petri dishes, and we'll be on our way home. *(Puts another under the microscope and looks at it.)*

SARAH: *(Moves about, looking at different items on the table.)* Working amidst all this clutter! I sometimes wonder how you can find your own gloves, no less some kind of germ killer.

ALEXANDER: Antibiotic.

SARAH: Whatever. *(Notices something.)* My, this is certainly a disgusting little item here.

ALEXANDER: *(Goes to her.)* What's that?

SARAH: It's kind of green... no, blue and... fuzzy. Quite disgusting!

ALEXANDER: *(Picks up the Petri dish.)* That's odd...

SARAH: It looks like mold on old bread.

ALEXANDER: It is mold. This Petri dish wasn't covered properly. So... oxygen got inside. But how...? *(Takes it over to the microscope.)*

SARAH: Can't this wait until tomorrow?

ALEXANDER: *(Looks through the microscope.)* This is interesting...

SARAH: Mold? Interesting?

MERLIN: *(ENTERS wearing a lab coat.)* Alexander?

ALEXANDER: *(Clearly excited.)* Pryce! Just the man!

MERLIN: I thought I heard voices in here. I wasn't expecting you until tomorrow. Good afternoon, Mrs. Fleming.

SARAH: Good afternoon, Dr. Pryce.

ALEXANDER: *(Still looks through the microscope.)* Pryce, you will not believe this...!

MERLIN: *(To SARAH.)* When did you return home from your holiday?

SARAH: We haven't been home yet. Alexander insisted we stop here first.

ALEXANDER: Take a look at this, Pryce!

MERLIN: *(Looks.)* I don't need a microscope to recognize mold when I see it! Disgusting stuff.

SARAH: That's what I say.

MERLIN: Did you grow it on purpose?

ALEXANDER: No, the lid on this Petri dish wasn't sealed properly.

MERLIN: You've always been a bit careless about things like that.

Mold Juice

ALEXANDER: Yes, that's true, but this time it was a good thing. Over the past two weeks, left in the dark and exposed to oxygen and humidity, mold started growing on this staph culture.

SARAH: Staph?

ALEXANDER: Staphylococci.

SARAH: Sounds horrible!

MERLIN: Actually, it is, Mrs. Fleming. Staph causes all sorts of infectious diseases.

SARAH: Well, close the lid this instant!

MERLIN: We take every precaution, Mrs. Fleming—

ALEXANDER: By our good fortune, this dish was left open and exposed to the air!

SARAH: Good fortune?!

MERLIN: I don't understand you, Doctor.

ALEXANDER: Come and look at this, Pryce, and see if you see what I see! *(MERLIN goes to ALEXANDER.)*

SARAH: Mold is what he'll see!

MERLIN: *(Looks through the microscope.)* The mold... seems to have... surrounded the staph culture... *(Looks up.)* And it seems to be spreading in a normal manner.

ALEXANDER: Yes! The mold! But look again!

MERLIN: *(Looks again into the microscope.)* The staph seems...

ALEXANDER: Yes! The staph!

MERLIN: *(Looks up.)* How large was this staph culture, Dr. Fleming?

ALEXANDER: It covered nearly the entire surface. But look at it now!

MERLIN: *(Back to the microscope.)* Why... now it's only a few centimeters in diameter.

ALEXANDER: Exactly!

MERLIN: Remarkable!

SARAH: Alexander, does that mean the staph is turning into mold?

ALEXANDER: Much, much better than that, my dear. *(To MERLIN.)* What would you say, Pryce?

MERLIN: *(Hesitates.)* Well... it appears that... the mold is... feeding off of the same substrate as the staph! It is, in essence, starving the staph, taking away its food source!

ALEXANDER: My thought as well! It will take further testing, but if mold can not only contain but actually destroy staphylococci—!

MERLIN: What a breakthrough!

ALEXANDER: It's easy enough to create mold! All the conditions were accidentally present in the room while I was gone—darkness, warmth, and humidity.

MERLIN: And an organism to grow on. In this case, the staph culture.

ALEXANDER: And oxygen. Though the lab was closed up for two weeks, so the ventilation was quite poor.

SARAH: But, Alexander, one of the windows was left halfway open. I noticed it when I pulled up the shades.

ALEXANDER: That would do it! All the necessary conditions to grow mold.

MERLIN: Exactly!

MRS. DOWNIE: *(ENTERS with a mop and pail of water. She is surprised to see people in the room.)* Oh, goodness gracious! I didn't know anyone was in here. I beg your pardon!

SARAH: Not your fault. Dr. Fleming decided to stop in a day early.

ALEXANDER: Mrs. Downie! Just the person I need to see!

MRS. DOWNIE: Me? I just came in to mop up before you got back—

ALEXANDER: Two questions, Mrs. Downie—two very important questions!

MRS. DOWNIE: Oh, me! I can't answer any kind of question you're likely to put to me, Dr. Fleming!

ALEXANDER: You can answer these! You must!

SARAH: Alexander, you're upsetting the poor woman.

MERLIN: It's quite all right, Mrs. Downie. You've done nothing wrong.

MRS. DOWNIE: I should hope not... *(Puts down the pail and mop.)*

ALEXANDER: First question. *(Holds the Petri dish before her.)* Did you, by accident or on purpose, open the lid of this Petri dish?

MRS. DOWNIE: Me? Touch one of those germ things? Not on my life! It's bad enough I have to come in here and mop up. I says to Matron just the other day—

ALEXANDER: *(To MERLIN.)* This is excellent! It means the culture has been exposed for at least two weeks. That's assuming no one else has entered this room—

MRS. DOWNIE: Matron don't let no one in here but me once a week.

ALEXANDER: Very good, Mrs. Downie. Now for my second question.

MRS. DOWNIE: Doctor?

ALEXANDER: By any chance, did you open that window over there. *(Points OFF.)*

MRS. DOWNIE: *(Hesitates.)* Ah... that one over there?

ALEXANDER: Yes. The one that is still open.

MRS. DOWNIE: Well...

SARAH: *(Comforts her.)* It's not all that important, Mrs. Downie.

ALEXANDER: Actually, it is, Sarah.

MERLIN: *(To MRS. DOWNIE.)* Dr. Alexander is just trying to establish the atmospheric condition of the room.

MRS. DOWNIE: The what?

ALEXANDER: Mrs. Downie, it is not a crime to open a window—

SARAH: I should say not! Stop frightening the woman, Alexander!

ALEXANDER: If you did open the window, Mrs. Downie, I would need to know when you did so and how long it has remained open. It is crucial!

MRS. DOWNIE: If you put it like that... Yes, I opened it. And two others as well. It was hot as blazes in here last week when I come in to mop up, so I opened them three windows. Afore I left, I shut them again. 'Cept I guess I missed one, the shades being down and all. I'm sorry, Dr. Alexander. You won't tell Matron, will you?

ALEXANDER: A week ago, you say?

MRS. DOWNIE: A week ago today, if you want the whole truth of the matter.

ALEXANDER: Pryce, do you see? The culture has only been exposed to fresh air—or what London considers fresh air—for a week. And look how far the mold has developed!

MERLIN: And how much of the staph has already been destroyed!

MRS. DOWNIE: *(Mutters.)* I'm sure to get the sack now.

SARAH: No one is going to sack you, Mrs. Downie.

MERLIN: Quite on the contrary, Mrs. Downie. You have been of invaluable assistance!

MRS. DOWNIE: Me?

ALEXANDER: Something very important has happened in this laboratory over the past two weeks.

MRS. DOWNIE: No goings-on in here, Doctor. It's been locked up tight. You have my word on that!

SARAH: Something to do with germs and mold in that Petri dish, Mrs. Downie. As I understand it, the mold that was formed because the lid was left open—

ALEXANDER: And the window was left open!

SARAH: That mold, it seems, kills certain germs.

MRS. DOWNIE: Kills germs!

ALEXANDER: Many tests have to be undertaken, but at this point, it appears that the secretions from the mold—call it... mold juice—may save lives! It attacks the germs that spread influenza, pneumonia—

MERLIN: Possibly typhoid—

ALEXANDER: Impossible to say how many other infectious diseases!

MRS. DOWNIE: That sounds all well and good, Doctor, but I don't think no sensible person is going to take no medicine called "mold juice." *(MERLIN, SARAH, and ALEXANDER laugh.)*

SARAH: She's got a point there, Alexander. "Mold juice" sounds positively disgusting!

ALEXANDER: I suppose we could use the scientific name. Pryce, what kind of mold would you classify this sample as?

MERLIN: Well... *(Looks into the microscope.)* It clearly looks like genus penicillin to me.

ALEXANDER: Exactly my observation. *(To MRS. DOWNIE and SARAH.)* What do you ladies say to the name penicillin?

SARAH: *(Thinks about it.)* Penicillin...

MRS. DOWNIE: Not as catchy as Grover's Liver Pills, but I'd give it a try. Penicillin. Sounds good. Just don't tell folks it's made of mold juice! *(ALL laugh as LIGHTS FADE to BLACK.)*

AFTERMATH

Alexander Fleming's discovery of "mold juice" was not immediately accepted by other scientists, and only after successful experiments by scientists from Great Britain to Australia was the drug's impact fully appreciated. In 1942, the first patient in the United States was treated successfully with penicillin. World War II quickly brought the antibiotic to the attention of the world as the healing powers of this miracle drug helped dramatically reduce the number of deaths and amputations to injured soldiers. Learning to mass-produce penicillin was challenging to laboratories until Pfizer, then a little-known chemical manufacturer, figured out how to make it in large volumes in 1943. On June 6, 1944, Allied soldiers carried penicillin from Pfizer with them onto the beaches at Normandy, and the drug is credited with saving thousands of lives in Europe between D-Day and Germany's surrender. In 1945, Fleming, along with the researchers from Oxford and Australia, were awarded a Nobel Prize for the discovery of penicillin. Since then, the antibiotic has saved millions of lives through its treatment of pneumonia, influenza, typhoid, and dozens of other infectious diseases. Today, Fleming's lab in St. Mary's Hospital in London is the Alexander Fleming Laboratory Museum. He died in 1955 at the age of 73.

GARAGE GUYS
(1939)

BACKGROUND

William Reddington Hewlett (1913-2001) was born in Ann Arbor, Michigan, the son of a medical professor. He received science and electrical engineering degrees from Stanford University and the Massachusetts Institute of Technology. While studying at Stanford with renowned scientist Dr. Frederick Terman, Hewlett started working on projects with David Packard (1912-1996).

Packard, the son of an attorney, was born in Pueblo, Colorado, and received undergraduate and graduate degrees in electrical engineering at Stanford. While Packard was finishing his degree, he and Hewlett worked together in Packard's home in Palo Alto, California, and in 1938, took out a patent on an audio oscillator that eliminated the negative feedback in recording devices and speakers. That same year, Packard married Lucile Salter.

CHARACTERS

DAVID PACKARD (M)............electrical engineer
LUCILE PACKARD (F)............his wife
BILL HEWLETT (M).................electrical engineering student

SETTING

Time: The evening of Sunday, January 1, 1939.
Place: David Packard's one-car detached garage at his house in Palo Alto, California.

SET DESCRIPTION

The garage has some of the usual items, such as tools hanging on the wall, spare tires, a push lawnmower, a garden hose, etc. There are also two tables covered with electrical equipment, including speakers, amplifiers, microphones, etc. Wires run from the equipment all over the floor. There are also two kitchen chairs. A single door is the only entrance other than the garage door. A single light bulb hangs from the ceiling.

PROPERTIES

Folder, envelope with papers, pen, coin (BILL).

SOUND EFFECTS

Static, piercing feedback, loud feedback screech.

LIGHTS UP on the garage. DAVID PACKARD sits at one of the tables, turning dials on one of the pieces of equipment. SOUND EFFECT: STATIC then PIERCING FEEDBACK. He adjusts the dials and the NOISE STOPS. He speaks into the microphone, and his voice is heard coming from the speakers.

DAVID: This is your host, David Packard, coming to you from the grand ballroom of the St. Francis Hotel in San Francisco— *(SOUND EFFECT: LOUD FEEDBACK SCREECH. He adjusts the dials again and the FEEDBACK STOPS.)* This is your engineer extraordinaire, David Packard, coming to you from his garage in Palo Alto, California— *(Again, SOUND EFFECT: LOUD FEEDBACK SCREECH. He quickly adjusts the dials, and the FEEDBACK STOPS as LUCILE ENTERS with BILL. She wears a housedress and an apron, and he wears casual attire and carries a folder.)*

LUCILE: Here he is, Bill, making that god-awful noise again.

BILL: Happy New Year, David. *(Goes to the table where DAVID continues to adjust the dials.)* When Lucile said you were out in the garage, I thought you were working on your car.

DAVID: No, my workshop has been condemned to the garage and our car to the alley. It was Lucile's idea.

LUCILE: It was our first argument. Married five months and finally our first argument.

DAVID: I thought it was our first fight.

LUCILE: No, David, dear. It was just an argument.

DAVID: Well, in any case, I lost.

BILL: Newlyweds!

LUCILE: Bill, he stays up all hours working on his contraption, and I'm trying to sleep in the next room.

DAVID: For months I've been explaining to her what we are doing, and still she calls it a contraption!

LUCILE: I know that it is an audio oscillator, and it not only converts DC, or direct current, to AC, or alternating current, but it also creates a square wave which produces frequencies in the audio range of approximately 16 hertz to 20 kilohertz. *(Beat.)* See? I have been paying attention. I just prefer to call it a contraption.

BILL: *(Laughs.)* Lucile, you are something else!

LUCILE: Well, whatever I am, I need my sleep. So, after a rather lively argument—

DAVID: Fight.

LUCILE: —we decided to move the workshop to the garage. Didn't Edison invent the light bulb in his garage?

BILL: *(Laughs.)* Maybe so, Lucile! *(Points to the bulb.)* In fact, I think that's the very one! We could use some more light in here.

LUCILE: You two are electrical engineers, aren't you? Surely you can figure out how to run an extension cord or two for extra light.

DAVID: Bill's the one making derogatory comments about the lighting. I'll let him figure it out.

LUCILE: There you go. Now I have to get back to the supper dishes. Make all the noise you want, David. The neighbors will think we're still celebrating New Year's Day. *(EXITS.)*

DAVID: My wife...

BILL: A smart girl.

DAVID: Don't I know it.

BILL: What's with all this noise? *(Sits next to DAVID at the table.)*

DAVID: I've been purposely allowing for negative feedback to see how the oscillator reacts. Our Model 200A is pretty effective, but I have a few ideas on how we can improve it.

BILL: Time for Model B?

DAVID: Maybe. The square wave periodically changes, just as we planned, but I think we can control it more.

BILL: That would allow for an even clearer recording device...

DAVID: And consequently, a higher quality sound from speakers that are designed to accept the better frequencies.

BILL: I think we better take out a patent on Model B as soon as we can test it and get it graphed. And the sooner the better.

DAVID: Why the urgency, Bill? Do you think someone else is onto this idea?

BILL: Not that I know of, but I have a better reason to get the best audio oscillator on the market.

DAVID: On the market? We're not even a company yet.

BILL: Yes, we are. Or we will be after tomorrow. *(Opens the folder and pulls out papers.)* I've been going over all the papers needed to become an actual company. It's not as difficult as it sounds. In fact, California is one of the easiest states to form a company.

DAVID: So, we become a company. I still don't understand the rush.

BILL: I got a phone call from Fred Terman yesterday.

DAVID: Dr. Terman?

BILL: My mentor, your current teacher, and the man who knows more about what is going on in the world of electronics than anyone else.

DAVID: He's been very encouraging. I've told him about our Model 200A audio oscillator. He seemed impressed. But with Terman, you can never quite tell.

BILL: Believe me, he's impressed. That's why he called me. It seems he was approached by a company that is looking for a state-of-the-art recording and speaking system, and of course, they went to Terman.

DAVID: Who called him?

BILL: Don't laugh, David.

DAVID: Laugh? This is a serious piece of news!

BILL: I know. So you mustn't laugh. The call was from Walt Disney. *(DAVID laughs.)* I knew you would laugh.

DAVID: Walt Disney! Mickey Mouse and Pluto, Snow White and those seven midgets—

BILL: Dwarfs, actually.

DAVID: <u>That</u> Walt Disney?

BILL: Yes, <u>that</u> Walt Disney. Now, if you will get serious, I will explain.

DAVID: *(Mocks.)* Let me guess! Donald Duck needs an audio oscillator so everyone can figure out what he is actually saying!

BILL: *(Scolds.)* David!

DAVID: Alright, alright. So, Walt Disney calls Terman. Why?

BILL: Disney has this big project in the works. A feature cartoon that is scored with classical music. He got the Philadelphia Orchestra to perform the pieces, and he got Leopold Stokowski to conduct it. This is high-class stuff. Disney wants a sound system that is superior to the conventional movie sound.

DAVID: This is for real?

BILL: So, what Disney is looking for is a state-of-the-art recording system and specially-made speakers for broadcasting the music in the movie theatre. Terman immediately thought of our work.

DAVID: What did he tell Disney?

BILL: That he would look into it and get back to him. That's why we have to become a company and be able to present Model B to Disney before he finds someone else.

DAVID: What about the start-up money, Bill? Lucile and I are just making ends meet with me still in school—

BILL: I told you I would take care of that. I got two banks interested enough to give us a loan, thanks to a recommendation by Terman.

DAVID: How much?

BILL: Five hundred thirty-eight dollars!

DAVID: Terrific! Then I say we fill out those papers and file them first thing Monday morning!

BILL: Exactly what I was thinking. I've filled out most of them. We are down as co-founders and directors. I'm using your home address as the location.

DAVID: I hope they don't find out we're in a garage.

BILL: What's the matter with a garage? Didn't Edison invent the light bulb in his garage? *(Both laugh.)* This sheet is about taxes, and this one's about employees' contracts—

DAVID: What employees?

BILL: Well, right now we only have two.

DAVID: I say we give them a raise!

BILL: Agreed. And this sheet is for later if we wish to open the company to shareholders.

DAVID: We should be so lucky.

BILL: It's all here. Except one thing.

DAVID: What's that?

BILL: The name of the company. You have to have an official name, and it cannot be changed without a lot of legal complications.

DAVID: So, we'll give it a name. *(Thinks.)* The California Electronics Company!

BILL: Too local.

DAVID: The American Electronics Company!

BILL: Think global!

DAVID: The International Electronics Company!

BILL: But it's more than electronics. There's no saying where this may lead.

DAVID: Universal Industries, Inc.!

BILL: David, think a moment. Bell Telephone. Ford Motor Company. Eastman Kodak. McDonnell Aircraft.

DAVID: You mean use our names?

BILL: Why not?

DAVID: Packard and Hewlett? Hewlett and Packard?

BILL: Get rid of the "and." It sounds too folksy.

DAVID: Packard-Hewlett. Hewlett-Packard.

BILL: Nice and simple. It could mean all kinds of products!

DAVID: But which name goes first?

BILL: Let's toss a coin. Heads, Packard goes first. Tails, Hewlett goes first.

DAVID: Sure. Let fate decide. You got any change?

BILL: *(Pulls a coin from his pocket.)* Here's a quarter. Here... *(Gives it to DAVID.)* ...you toss.

DAVID: Okay. *(Takes the coin.)* Here goes. *(Tosses the coin, catches it, and looks at it.)* Tails. It's Hewlett-Packard.

BILL: No hard feelings?

DAVID: Hey, I got my name on a real live company! *(Writes on the document.)* "Hewlett-Packard." Now let's sign this thing!

BILL: It's got to be witnessed.

DAVID: Lucile can do it. *(Calls OFF.)* Lucile! Can you come out here for a minute, please? *(To BILL.)* A relation is legal, isn't it?

BILL: Very legal.

LUCILE: *(ENTERS.)* What is it, David?

DAVID: Lucile, would you witness this document for us? Bill and I are finally making it official. We're a company!

LUCILE: And about time, too.

DAVID: *(Signs.)* I am signing as the co-founder... *(Hands paper to BILL.)* And Bill signs there... *(BILL signs.)*

LUCILE: Oh, this is exciting! An actual company!

BILL: This is the real thing, alright.

DAVID: Now, Lucile... *(Hands her the pen.)* ...you sign right there where it reads "witnessed by." Then write in the date.

BILL: January 1, 1939. The start of a great year!

LUCILE: *(Reads the paper.)* You're calling the company Hewlett-Packard?

DAVID: Ah... yes.

LUCILE: Not Packard-Hewlett?

BILL: *(Hesitates.)* Well, ah...

DAVID: *(Gets an idea.)* We did a marketing study. Looked up what looked best on paper, the letters that catch one's eye, the advantages of the initials HP over PH, and the impact—

LUCILE: All right! I didn't want a dissertation. *(Signs the paper.)* If I were you two, I would have just tossed a coin to see whose name goes first. *(LIGHTS FADE to BLACK.)*

AFTERMATH

The first major project for the newly formed Hewlett-Packard Company was providing several HP 200 Model B audio oscillators and speakers for the recording of Disney's *Fantasia* in 1940. Hewlett-Packard also provided special speakers for the initial showings of the movie in New York and Los Angeles. HP, as it soon came to be known, quickly grew into a major name in electronics and by 1957, offered shares in the company. It would become a leading manufacturer of television components, computers, printers, video games, and many other electronic machines.

William Hewlett served in World War II, was CEO of HP for several years, and in his later years, was a noted philanthropist with his wife. David Packard was the first president of HP, and years later, served as the United States Deputy Secretary of Defense under President Richard Nixon. Like Hewlett, he was a noteworthy philanthropist. Packard died in 1996 at the age of 83, and Hewlett died in 2001 at the age of 87.

Today, the Packard garage at 367 Addison Avenue in Palo Alto is an official California Historical Landmark. A plaque on the site calls it "the birthplace of Silicon Valley."

THE MOVIE STAR AND THE COMPOSER
(1942)

BACKGROUND

Hedy Lamarr was born Hedwig Eva Maria Kiesler in Vienna in 1914, and in her teens she became a celebrated beauty of European movies. She was brought to Hollywood in 1938 and enjoyed a long career starring in a variety of films. Although Lamarr was not educated in the sciences, she was an amateur inventor and assisted aviator-millionaire Howard Hughes in designing his planes, suggesting a streamlined structure to cut down on wind resistance.

George Antheil was born in 1900 in Trenton, New Jersey, and at a young age showed talent for playing and composing music. He spent much of his formative years in Europe with the avant-garde composers, poets, and painters of the 1920s, soon developing a radical style of music using bells, whistles, sirens, and other objects in his orchestrations. Antheil was soon dubbed "the bad boy of music." In 1936, he began writing more conventional scores for Hollywood movies even as he continued to experiment with music and pursue his interest in science. It was this interest that brought Antheil and Lamarr together in 1941 to work on a science project dealing with radio frequency.

CHARACTERS

CAPTAIN FORREST* (M) .... mature U.S. Naval officer
LIEUTENANT COMMANDER
    RUSSO* (M) .... young U.S. Naval officer
HEDY LAMARR (F) .... Austrian-born, glamorous Hollywood movie star
GEORGE ANTHEIL (M) .... American avant-garde composer

*Fictional characters

SETTING

Time: Late on a Tuesday morning in September 1942.
Place: A conference room in the headquarters of the U.S. Navy in Washington, D.C.

SET DESCRIPTION

The conference room is simple and stark with no windows. There is a large table littered with papers and files, with six chairs around it. A wastepaper basket is in the corner.

PROPERTIES

File filled with papers (HEDY).

The Movie Star and the Composer

LIGHTS UP on the conference room. CAPTAIN FORREST and LIEUTENANT COMMANDER RUSSO are in dress uniform and sit at one end of the table going through files together.

CAPTAIN: Another dead end. *(Tosses a file onto a pile of others.)* These proposals only have one thing in common.

LIEUTENANT: What's that, Captain?

CAPTAIN: Too expensive. Time-consuming and expensive. And the chance of success minimal. I could find the money if it was worth it, but I don't have the time. This war isn't going to last forever!

LIEUTENANT: I certainly hope not, Captain.

CAPTAIN: Every time one of those convoys leaves the base, no matter what kind of escort we give them, by the time they are halfway across the Atlantic—or the Pacific—they're nothing but...

LIEUTENANT: Sitting ducks?

CAPTAIN: Exactly. *(Picks up a file.)* And half-cocked proposals like this are not going to help. *(Looks at his watch.)* How about an early lunch before we start going over those lab results? *(Rises.)*

LIEUTENANT: But, Captain Forrest, sir...

CAPTAIN: What is it, Russo?

LIEUTENANT: You promised you would see Mrs. Markey and Mr. Antheil today. They've been waiting all morning.

CAPTAIN: Markey? Antheil?

LIEUTENANT: Markey is her married name. It's actually Hedy Lamarr.

CAPTAIN: The movie star? Send her to Sanders. He handles all the USO stuff.

LIEUTENANT: She's not here about entertaining the troops, though she does that as well.

CAPTAIN: What's she want to see me for?

LIEUTENANT: About a defense mechanism. Evidently, she and Mr. Anthiel have received a patent—

CAPTAIN: And who's this Anthiel? A movie director?

LIEUTENANT: No, Captain. A... composer.

CAPTAIN: A songwriter? "Praise the Lord and Pass the Ammunition." That sort of thing?

LIEUTENANT: Far from it, sir. He composes very... strange music. They call it "avant-garde," I believe. Not the sort of thing you'd hear on the radio, at least not on *Your Hit Parade*.

CAPTAIN: Lieutenant Commander Russo, are you telling me there is a screen pin-up girl and an artsy composer waiting out there to talk to me about defense?

LIEUTENANT: That is precisely the case, Captain.

CAPTAIN: McGinley should have screened them and got them out of here!

LIEUTENANT: Sergeant McGinley did see them, sir, and looked at their patent. And he thinks you should hear what they have to say.

CAPTAIN: Of all the fool things—!

LIEUTENANT: Should I bring them in, Captain?

CAPTAIN: Might as well. Otherwise, it sounds like it will take a couple of MPs to get rid of them!

LIEUTENANT: Yes, sir. *(EXITS and CAPTAIN sits.)*

CAPTAIN: Hedy Lamarr! What next? Betty Grable will come in with plans for a pink submarine?

LIEUTENANT: *(ENTERS followed by HEDY LAMARR and GEORGE ANTHEIL. HEDY wears a practical skirt and jacket and has her hair pulled back. She carries a thick file. ANTHEIL wears a casual jacket and tie.)* Captain Forrest, Mrs. Markey and Mr. Antheil.

CAPTAIN: Come in, come in. *(Points to the other side of the table.)* Sit here... and here.

HEDY: Thank you for seeing us, Captain. *(Sits with GEORGE.)*

CAPTAIN: *(Sits.)* Sure, sure. *(LIEUTENANT remains standing behind them.)* So, I hear you have some kind of patent?

HEDY: Yes.

GEORGE: It was just approved last month by the U.S. Patent Office. It has to do with radio frequency.

CAPTAIN: Well, the Navy has its own people working on that, and they have made some encouraging progress. Top scientists. Very well qualified for this kind of work.

HEDY: We are not—as you say, Captain—top scientists, but Mr. Anthiel and I have been working together over the past year—

CAPTAIN: A whole year. Imagine that.

HEDY: Yes. And over that period of time, we have developed a system of frequency hopping—

CAPTAIN: Frequency hopping. That doesn't sound very scientific to me.

GEORGE: *(Gets testy.)* You may call it anything you like! It works!

HEDY: Please, George. We must make ourselves perfectly clear.

CAPTAIN: Yes. Please do.

HEDY: Captain, Mr. Anthiel and I have… unique experience in our own individual way. Together we—

CAPTAIN: And what kind of experience is that, Mrs. Markey? University degrees in science? Employment in technical research and development? Lab experience with recognized scientific organizations?

HEDY: No.

CAPTAIN: I thought not.

HEDY: My first husband back in Austria was a munitions manufacturer. I know a great deal about torpedoes. German torpedoes. I also worked with Mr. Howard Hughes and learned about aerial engineering and aviation radio.

CAPTAIN: And you, Mr. Anthiel?

GEORGE: I am a composer—

CAPTAIN: How commendable—

GEORGE: —which means I am a mathematician. I study numbers, and I understand frequency and sound.

HEDY: As I said, captain, with these kinds of talents combined we have been successful in—

CAPTAIN: *(Rises.)* I am sorry, Mrs. Markey, but I am a very busy man. You two obviously lack the credentials for the United States Navy to take seriously—

HEDY: *(Rises.)* Members of the Navy are dying by the hundreds every day! As well as those in the Army and the Marines! Axis torpedoes are killing them, and we have a system that just may be able to stop them! This is a war, Captain! Not a time to worry about credentials and resumes and university degrees! We are not applying for jobs! We are here to help, and it is your job as an officer and an American to give us a few minutes to listen to our plan!

CAPTAIN: *(Contemplates.)* All right. *(Sits.)* Explain yourselves.

HEDY: George, perhaps you can start. *(Sits.)*

GEORGE: Glad to. *(Opens up the folder and spreads out sheets on the table.)* These are frequency charts, but they only tell half the story. *(LIEUTENANT comes to the table and looks as well.)* As you know, the Axis torpedo is radio-controlled. Currently, our ships can detect the radio signals but can't do anything about it because it is too late to move out of the torpedo's predetermined path. This is where the frequency hopping comes in. If one of our radio operators can jam the radio signals being sent to the torpedo, it will be confused and lose its path.

LIEUTENANT: But the enemy will quickly pick up on this frequency and override it.

HEDY: That is where frequency hopping comes in. The radio signals would be quickly and randomly changed, causing further jamming and making the enemy unable to determine the new frequency.

LIEUTENANT: How many frequencies are possible?

GEORGE: Countless! *(Rises and leans over the table, pointing to the sheets.)* But I have developed a system with 88 frequencies.

LIEUTENANT: Why 88?

HEDY: The piano! There are 88 black and white keys on the piano.

CAPTAIN: *(Scowls.)* A piano! What next!

GEORGE: The idea came from the piano. Do you remember the old piano rolls? The paper ones with the holes in it?

CAPTAIN: Nobody uses those any more—

LIEUTENANT: I remember them! My parents still have lots of them.

GEORGE: The holes in the paper indicated which of the 88 keys were to be struck. I used the same idea for frequency hopping! Random holes in the signaling device with infinite possibilities. Just as there are millions of different songs that can be played on one piano, so too, there are countless possibilities in frequency hopping!

LIEUTENANT: I see!

HEDY: By jamming the radio signals, the torpedoes will change course once, twice—who is to say how many times—but the chances of it hitting its intended target is very slight.

GEORGE: An estimated nine percent.

LIEUTENANT: I like those odds.

GEORGE: There is also the possibility that the jamming will cause the torpedo to stop functioning altogether. Its propeller would freeze up, and it would sink to the bottom of the ocean.

HEDY: I know my first husband was very concerned with the various ways in which a radio torpedo could be disabled. These torpedoes are deadly, but they are also very fragile when it comes to radio interference.

LIEUTENANT: *(Looks closer at the plans.)* Interesting...

CAPTAIN: Yes, yes. All very interesting. *(Rises.)* You leave these papers with us, and I'll see that they are given a thorough looking over.

HEDY: *(Contains her frustration.)* I appreciate that, Captain. *(Rises.)*

GEORGE: *(Wilts.)* Yeah... sure...

CAPTAIN: *(Gathers up the papers in the file.)* Thank you both for coming in.

LIEUTENANT: Yes. Thank you, Miss Lamarr—I mean Mrs. Markey. And Mr. Antheil.

HEDY: You are welcome. *(Starts to leave.)* Oh, Captain...

CAPTAIN: Yes, Mrs. Markey?

HEDY: You will be careful with that file, won't you?

CAPTAIN: Careful?

HEDY: Regard it as top secret. If those plans should fall into enemy hands, it would be disastrous.

CAPTAIN: Oh, yes. Very careful. Top secret.

HEDY: Good day... *(EXITS with GEORGE.)*

LIEUTENANT: Remarkable woman... *(CAPTAIN frowns.)* ... for a movie star.

CAPTAIN: *(Growls.)* A system based on a player piano! That's what we need to win this war. *(Tosses the file into the wastepaper basket.)* I'm going to lunch. *(To himself.)* Eighty-eight keys... *(EXITS. LIEUTENANT slowly goes to the basket and pulls out the file. He studies it as LIGHTS FADE to BLACK.)*

AFTERMATH

George Antheil continued to compose operas, ballets, and orchestral pieces until his death in 1959 of a heart attack at the age of 59. Hedy Lamarr continued to perform in movies and television until her retirement in 1958. She died in 2000.

The U.S. Navy did not pursue Lamarr and Anthiel's frequency hopping invention during World War II. The file was finally studied and implemented in 1962 during the blockage of Cuba by the U.S. Navy. Lamarr and Anthiel's contribution to the invention of frequency hopping was not recognized until decades after World War II and served as the basis for other scientific developments, including Bluetooth and COFDM used in Wi-Fi systems. Both Lamarr and Anthiel were posthumously inducted into the Inventors Hall of Fame in 2014.

DECODING THE DOLL WOMAN
(1944)

BACKGROUND

Elizebeth Smith Friedman (1892-1980) was America's first and foremost woman cryptologist, breaking codes for various U.S. government agencies for 25 years. She was born Elizebeth Smith in Huntington, Indiana, where she grew up on a farm. In college, she showed a proficiency for languages and a fascination with Shakespeare's works. Elizebeth was hired by textile millionaire Colonel George Fabyan to work at his Riverbank Laboratories. Her job was to go through the works of William Shakespeare and find hidden codes and messages to prove that they were written by Francis Bacon. At Riverside, Elizebeth met and married William Friedman, who was also a cryptologist. During Prohibition, Elizebeth left Riverside and was hired by the U.S. Treasury Department to decipher the codes bootleggers and rum runners were using to smuggle alcohol and other goods into the country. She decoded thousands of messages and was in such demand that Elizebeth eventually worked for the U.S. Coast Guard, the Bureau of Narcotics, the Bureau of Internal Revenue, the Department of Justice, and other agencies. Before America entered World War II, she decoded a series of transmissions from Nazi spies in South America about a planned attack on the United States from the south that was later abandoned by the Germans.

CHARACTERS

AGENT GLEN
    MORTON* (M) .... of the FBI
MAJOR FRED
    BRADSHAW* (M) .... Navy officer
ELIZEBETH SMITH
    FRIEDMAN (F) .... cryptologist

*Fictional characters

SETTING

Time: Early morning on January 21, 1944.
Place: An office in the FBI headquarters, Washington D.C.

SET DESCRIPTION

Agent Glen Morton's office is small and cluttered. There is a desk and chair, two folding chairs for guests, and a row of file cabinets. There are papers and files everywhere and a phone, notepad, and pen on the desk.

PROPERTIES

Folder filled with papers and letters, purse (ELIZEBETH).

LIGHTS UP on the FBI office. AGENT GLEN MORTON sits at his desk and talks on the phone. His jacket hangs on the back of the chair, his tie is loosened, and his shirt sleeves are rolled up.

MORTON: That ain't enough, Gordie. The money looks suspicious, I know, but there could be a legit explanation. *(Listens.)* If you bring her in, I'm afraid her contacts will disappear. I need more solid stuff. *(Listens.)* Yeah, you might be right. Where is she now? *(Listens.)* Well, have your man keep on her. I might have something for you real soon. *(Listens.)* The Navy thinks they got the goods on her. *(Listens.)* I'm expecting them any second, so stay near the phone— *(MAJOR FRED BRADSHAW ENTERS with ELIZEBETH. He is in a naval uniform and removes his hat. She is dressed in a practical dress suit and hat and carries a purse and a thick folder.)*

MAJOR: Glen?

MORTON: *(Into the phone.)* They're here now. So long, Gordie. *(Rises and goes to MAJOR.)* Fred! *(Shakes his hand.)* They didn't say it would be you! They just told me Navy.

MAJOR: That's me. Navy. *(To ELIZEBETH.)* Glen Morton. We go way back together. *(To MORTON.)* Do you know Mrs. Friedman?

MORTON: *(Hesitates.)* Uh...

MAJOR: Elizebeth Smith Friedman?

MORTON: *(Realizes.)* I should say so! I mean, we haven't met... *(Shakes her hand.)* ...but I sure have heard a lot about you, Mrs. Friedman. You're the one that nailed the Ezra brothers!

ELIZEBETH: Well...

MORTON: I don't mean it like that, ma'am, but you decoded all their stuff. Nasty guys, the Ezra brothers. Narcotics smuggling, big time. Hey, have a seat, both of you. *(Returns to his desk and puts on his jacket as they sit in the chairs.)* Look at me! I look like a bum, and I got a lady in the office.

ELIZEBETH: Don't bother on my account. It is rather warm in here.

MORTON: It's January. We got the same boiler as the White House. Roosevelt gets a chill so they turn up the heat, and we all sweat. So, Fred, I hear you got something we can use on the Doll Woman case.

MAJOR: Mrs. Friedman is working for the Navy these days—

MORTON: Yeah. I heard all about that South America thing. Remarkable!

MAJOR: That was top secret!

MORTON: Fred, you're talking to the FBI! *(To ELIZEBETH.)* The messages you decoded from those Nazi spies in Brazil, Mrs. Friedman—unbelievable stuff!

ELIZEBETH: It was my first experience with the German Enigma machine. I learned a lot.

MORTON: I'll bet you did. And I'm hoping you learned something about this Dickinson woman.

ELIZEBETH: The so-called Doll Woman?

MORTON: Yeah, I gave her that name. But she ain't no doll, if you know what I mean. *(Picks up a photo from his desk and shows it to them.)* Valvalee Dickinson. Not much to look at. If she's a spy, she ain't no Mata Hari.

ELIZEBETH: Oh, she's a spy alright.

MORTON: *(Rises.)* You say so? You got the goods?

MAJOR: Settle down, Glen.

MORTON: I need to know! I got two men trailing this Dickinson woman in New York City right now!

MAJOR: What's the FBI got on her?

MORTON: Just money stuff. Lots of money. *(Sits.)* She was receiving payments from some Japanese businessmen from 1937 until Pearl Harbor. The money was all handled through Dickinson's antique doll shop on Madison Avenue and the payments look legit. These real old dolls go for a lot of money, and people buy them as an investment. She sold dolls to lots of people all over the world until the war broke out. *(Opens a file.)* I got ahold of lots of bills of sale and whatnot.

ELIZEBETH: So what makes you suspect Valvalee Dickinson is a spy, Mr. Morton?

MORTON: All those Japanese customers left the country one week before Pearl Harbor was attacked, and when we followed up on some of her customers in South America—a lot in Brazil—it turned out they didn't exist. Phony names using post office addresses.

MAJOR: Well, the Navy had a bit of luck. One of those phony names was in San Francisco, and the post office box had expired. The letters were about to be returned, but Dickinson changed the location of her doll shop in October of 1941. It was only a block away on Madison Avenue, but the letters got held up at the New York City post office. By December and the Pearl Harbor attack, the letters caught somebody's eye and were sent to the police, who sent them on to us.

MORTON: *(Rises.)* They should have contacted the FBI!

MAJOR: Bureaucracy, Glen. Pure bureaucracy. I didn't see the letters until two weeks ago, and I immediately called on Mrs. Friedman.

MORTON: What was so suspicious about a pile of unopened letters that even a postal clerk would notice?

ELIZEBETH: They were all addressed to different names with the same P.O. Box number.

MAJOR: And all the names were Japanese.

MORTON: Hmm. So, what's in the letters?

MAJOR: On the surface they are correspondences in English from Valvalee Dickinson to various customers about the sale of different dolls.

MORTON: That's no help to me. *(Sits.)*

ELIZEBETH: Mr. Morton, the letters are very specific and descriptive about the dolls. Their quality, their condition, the suggested repairs, even the manufacturers' marks. It was clear to me right away that the letters were coded messages.

MAJOR: Dickinson was passing on vital information about the U.S. Naval ships to Japanese contacts in San Francisco.

MORTON: How did you know the letters were about the Navy if they just talked about dolls?

MAJOR: Because Mrs. Friedman broke the code!

MORTON: Well, I'll be!

MAJOR: Show him some of the letters, Mrs. Friedman.

ELIZEBETH: Certainly, Major. *(Opens her folder on the desk and pulls out papers and letters.)* The word "doll" refers to a ship. I figured that out quickly because the names of several of the dolls matched those of Navy vessels. After I did some research into antique dolls, other words and phrases fell into place. A Kestner doll, for example, is a destroyer. A Heubach doll is a battleship, a Kammer & Reinhardt doll is an aircraft carrier—

MORTON: How come they all got German names?

ELIZEBETH: Because the best dolls from the nineteenth century were all made in Germany, though the Armand Marseille doll comes from France and means a submarine. Then you have descriptive phrases about the dolls. A bisque doll means the ship is fully operational. A wax doll means it is not fully staffed. A doll with an articulated body is a ship at sea while a closed mouth doll is a ship at port. A doll with sleep eyes is a ship in dry dock. And on and on. *(Takes a letter.)* So, here is an example. *(Reads.)* "I have just acquired a Kammer & Reinhardt bisque doll from 1877 that I think you will like. She is a costumed doll named Sara and wears a Roman toga. She has a fully articulated body and is quite charming. I am expecting her to arrive on Tuesday. I will be happy to hold her for you if you are interested. The price is seventy-five dollars."

MAJOR: Translate that for Mr. Morton, if you please.

ELIZABETH: Valvalee Dickinson is telling her San Francisco contact that the aircraft carrier Saratoga is fully operational and fully staffed and is at sea but will be arriving at port on Tuesday. That was five days before the attack on Pearl Harbor.

MORTON: Remarkable!

ELIZABETH: Not all of the letters are able to include the name of the ship but offered more details. Take this one, for example. *(Picks up a letter and reads.)* "I know you have been looking for a Heubach doll in mint condition." *(To MORTON.)* Mint condition means a recently built ship. *(Reads.)* "I have found one with sleep eyes, a swivel head, ball and socket jointed limbs, a flange neck, and molded hair. She is quite a beautiful doll made around 1840 in Mare. The dress dates to the 1890s. I believe I can get a matching sister doll, but I cannot guarantee it. Let me know if you are interested. The price is one hundred dollars."

MORTON: What does all that mean?

ELIZABETH: Dickinson has somehow gotten word that a new battleship is near completion at the Mare Island Naval Shipyard. It has four triple-14 guns that turn—the swivel head—and eight twin 38-caliber guns—that's the ball and socket. The flange neck refers to the turret face and the molded hair to the two torpedo tubes. Dickinson believes there might be a sister ship but cannot confirm it. *(Sits.)*

MORTON: And all this information was being sent to Japan?

MAJOR: That was the intention, but these particular letters were never received. *(Sits.)*

MORTON: And you say you got a whole pile of them?

MAJOR: Twenty-two, to be exact. And all have been decoded by Mrs. Friedman here. The information in the letters matches naval records for the years 1937 to 1941.

MORTON: And you're sure they were written by the Doll Woman?

ELIZEBETH: They are typed, but the hand-written addresses and the signatures can be identified. And all are postmarked at the New York City post office close to her shop on Madison Avenue.

MORTON: That's enough for me. *(Picks up the phone and quickly dials.)* Fourteen thousand dollars for dolls!

MAJOR: What's that, Glen?

MORTON: Those Japanese businessmen paid her fourteen thousand bucks! Now we know it wasn't for dolls! *(Into the phone.)* Gordie? Bring her in! *(Listens.)* Yeah. And get an injunction to get to her safe deposit box at the bank. *(Listens.)* Okay. *(Hangs up.)* I knew there was something fishy about the Doll Woman.

ELIZEBETH: Does she still have the doll shop in Manhattan?

MORTON: She sure does. But since the beginning of the war, she doesn't make international sales, just walk-in trade.

MAJOR: In other words, no letters.

MORTON: Exactly.

MAJOR: My guess is that after Pearl Harbor, her Japanese contacts did not find her necessary anymore and dropped her.

MORTON: Could be. But while she was working for them, the Doll Woman was well paid. I'm curious to see how much she has in that safe deposit box of hers.

ELIZEBETH: Using the antique doll trade to get coded messages to the enemy is quite ingenious. It is not a difficult code to learn and use. I'm afraid it might be in use elsewhere.

MAJOR: Good point, Mrs. Friedman.

MORTON: I can alert the censor division here at the FBI to consider all correspondence regarding antique dolls as suspect.

MAJOR: I can do likewise with the Navy and have my superiors pass the word on to the Secretary of War.

MORTON: *(Laughs.)* It's a good thing Roosevelt only collects antique model ships and not dolls, or we'd be snooping into his correspondence!

ELIZEBETH: If you two do run across anything suspicious, I'd be happy to take a look at it.

MAJOR: You'd be the first person we call, Mrs. Friedman.

ELIZEBETH: *(Stands up.)* In the meantime, I have work to do. *(MORTON and MAJOR stand, and she shakes MORTON'S hand.)* Nice meeting you, Mr. Morton.

MORTON: And a thrill to meet you, Mrs. Friedman! You sure got those Ezra bothers! And now this! What's next?

MAJOR: I'm afraid that's top secret.

MORTON: *(Smiles.)* Argentina, I hear.

MAJOR: *(Bristles.)* Who told you that?

MORTON: *(Laughs.)* Ah, Fred! This is the FBI! *(To ELIZEBETH.)* With the Germans on the run, I hear Argentina is crawling with Nazis.

ELIZEBETH: That's what I understand from the Enigma machine.

MORTON: Well, you keep up the good work, Mrs. Friedman. With minds like yours working for us, I feel like we know what is really going on.

ELIZEBETH: Thank you, Mr. Morton. Goodbye. *(The phone rings.)*

MORTON: Hold on a second. *(Quickly picks up the phone.)* Gordie? *(Listens.)* Where? *(Listens.)* No kidding! *(Listens.)* Give me the details. *(Writes on a paper on his desk.)* Well, ain't that something? Good work, Gordie. I'll contact the New York office right away. *(Hangs up and laughs.)*

MAJOR: Well?

MORTON: They got her! *(Laughs.)* The Doll Woman was at the bank opening her safe deposit box!

MAJOR: What was inside?

MORTON: Eighteen thousand bucks in cash and a rare antique doll she says is worth over twelve hundred dollars! *(Laughs as he reads his note.)* "A Kestner bisque doll circa 1801."

ELIZEBETH: A destroyer, fully equipped.

MORTON: Yeah! *(ALL laugh as LIGHTS FADE to BLACK.)*

AFTERMATH

Valvalee Dickinson was found guilty of espionage by the U.S. District Court of New York in 1944. With a plea bargain, she was sentenced to ten years in federal prison and a fine of $10,000. Dickinson was paroled in 1951, changed her name, and was little heard of again. It is believed she died in 1980.

Elizebeth Friedman continued to work for the U.S. Navy but retired after the war, though she continued to consult for various agencies. She and her husband returned to the work that had first brought them together, studying the ciphers and hidden messages in the plays and poems of Shakespeare. The result was the award-winning book *The Shakespearean Ciphers Examined* which, ironically, proved that Francis Bacon did not write Shakespeare's works. William Friedman died in 1969 and is buried in Arlington Cemetery. Elizebeth Friedman died in 1980 at the age of 88. Her body was cremated, and the ashes were spread over her husband's grave in Arlington.

FEEDING THE ENEMY
(1951)

BACKGROUND

Louis Tompkins Wright (1891-1952) was one of the first Blacks to graduate from Harvard Medical School. During World War I, he was gassed and contracted tuberculosis, but still went on to have a brilliant career as a surgeon and medical researcher at Harlem Hospital. Wright was also active in the fight against segregation and a leader in the early years of the civil rights movement.

Both of Louis Wright's daughters also became physicians and researchers. Jane C. Wright (1919-2013) was a biochemist whose work in cancer research in the 1950s led to the effective use of chemotherapy, a treatment that has saved millions of lives over the decades. She was educated at Smith College where she first studied art, but soon turned to medicine and studied at the New York Medical College. After her internship at Bellevue Hospital, she went to Harlem Hospital as a physician. By 1950, Jane Wright was fully involved in cancer research at the Harlem Hospital Research Center, which was run by her father. By this time, however, he was getting too weak from his continued health issues to both administer the program and continue his research.

CHARACTERS

JANE C. WRIGHT (F) .... young biochemist
LOUIS TOMPKINS
    WRIGHT (M) .... her father; director of
                                       the Research Center

SETTING

Time: November, 1951.

Place: A laboratory in the Harlem Hospital Research Center, New York City.

SET DESCRIPTION

The laboratory is small. There is a long table filled with various glass containers, two microscopes, stacks of Petri dishes, notebooks, etc. Cabinets and shelves are also filled with similar research equipment. Three stools line the table. An overcoat and hat hang on a coat rack.

PROPERTIES

Overcoat, hat, handkerchief (LOUIS).

LIGHTS UP on the small laboratory. JANE WRIGHT sits on a stool looking into a microscope. She wears a lab coat over a simple dark dress. COUGHING is heard OFFSTAGE.

JANE: *(Without looking up.)* I hear you out there, Dad. Come on in and stop lingering in the hall. *(LOUIS WRIGHT COUGHS from OFFSTAGE and then ENTERS. He is dressed in a three-piece suit and carries his overcoat and hat.)*

JANE/LOUIS: What are you doing here so late?

LOUIS: I asked you first.

JANE: Actually, we asked each other at the same time.

LOUIS: I'm the elder, Jane, so, you have to answer first. *(Coughs.)*

JANE: Okay. *(Goes to him.)* About an hour ago, I was just thinking about putting on my coat and going home, but something caught my eye and it won't let go. Now what about you, Dad? You know this cold night air isn't good for you. You should be out of here and home before it gets dark. Doctor's orders.

LOUIS: What doctor?

JANE: This doctor. *(Tries to put his coat on him.)* Let me help you get your coat on—

LOUIS: *(Moves away from her over to the microscope as she's left holding his coat.)* Isn't David home all by himself waiting for you? *(Coughs.)*

JANE: I telephoned him at his office.

LOUIS: What law firm stays open this late?

JANE: Not that office. The job corps one. It turns out he's working late too. Getting these kids off the streets and into jobs is a 24-hour gig.

LOUIS: Jane, I like your David. *(Coughs.)*

JANE: So do I. But, Dad, that doesn't explain what you're doing here so late. Listen to you. You ought to be home in bed.

LOUIS: All my life, if I listened every time a doctor or a wife or a… daughter said, "You ought to be home in bed," I'd have spent most of my time in a horizontal position! *(Has a coughing fit, takes out a handkerchief, and coughs into it. JANE helps him sit on a stool.)*

JANE: I don't know about horizontal, but you are going to sit right here! *(He stops coughing and lowers the handkerchief to reveal blood.)* Oh, Dad… It's bad today?

LOUIS: Every day. But I can't stop. There's still too much to do. Here. And other places. Jane, did I tell you about my meeting with that young Dr. King?

JANE: Yes. I'd love to meet him.

LOUIS: Not a medical man. A doctor of religion. Oh, a whole lot more than religion! It's like he sees it all! The future— *(In his excitement, he starts coughing again.)*

JANE: Don't excite yourself, Dad. Take some deep breaths.

LOUIS: *(Stops coughing.)* I don't believe I've taken a true, healthy deep breath since the war. It was the gas… that awful gas.

JANE: I know, Dad.

LOUIS: And do you know what I've had ever since?

JANE: Tuberculosis, Dad. I know.

LOUIS: What I've had is a powerful streak of stubbornness that reminds me every day that there is work to be done! *(Rises and crosses over to her microscope.)*

JANE: *(Laughs.)* Stubbornness. You certainly have that, too.

LOUIS: Now what I want to know, Jane, is what caught your eye and kept you from going home at a decent hour.

JANE: Something interesting. Exciting, even. But I don't want you to get overexcited.

LOUIS: You've come up with something interesting, and you want me to just stand here and yawn?

JANE: Actually, I want you to sit. *(Helps him sit on the stool in front of her microscope.)* There.

LOUIS: So, what have you been up to, Jane?

JANE: I was returning to some of the old files on chemotherapy—

LOUIS: *(Wilts.)* Oh. The two of us spent so much time on chemotherapy. Years!

JANE: Three, to be precise.

LOUIS: Three years. And chemo is still considered dangerous. A last resort. No one understands it, and no one uses it. *(Coughs.)*

JANE: Only because the drugs used are unreliable. There are too many variables. The purpose is to destroy cancer cells, but there was no controlling it.

LOUIS: Like the old saying, the cure was sometimes worse than the disease. Sometimes with chemotherapy, it's true.

JANE: I was going through old experiments, looking at various patterns, even trying to connect what the failed cases had in common.

LOUIS: Death.

JANE: Stop being so negative, Dad, and listen to me.

LOUIS: I'm sorry. What did they have in common?

JANE: The drugs we used added protein to the cancer cells. Sometimes, they actually helped create new strands of DNA and RNA.

LOUIS: In other words, they were feeding the enemy.

JANE: Exactly! So I looked at some agents that had been tested for other reasons and found that nitrogen mustard did not, as you say, feed the enemy.

LOUIS: Nitrogen mustard! I believe that was in the gas they used in the First World War. The very chemical that destroyed my lungs!

JANE: We don't know exactly what the Germans put in those gases.

LOUIS: I don't think the Germans knew!

JANE: But studies show that nitrogen mustard fights folic acid. Without folic acid, cancer cells cannot produce the amino acids that allow for mitosis, and mitosis in cancer cells is much more rapid than in healthy cells in the human body.

LOUIS: Thus, the appalling rate in which various kinds of cancer can spread.

JANE: So, anything that is antagonistic to folic acid can—in theory—stop cancer cells from reproducing. And, if perfected, there is a chance that the cancer cells can be destroyed!

LOUIS: Jane, this is remarkable! Can it be done?

JANE: There are several steps that must be taken. The nitrogen mustard must be tested on actual tumors. If you look in my microscope, you can see how the anti-folic acid agents have stopped the mitosis process. *(LOUIS looks.)* But that is not an actual cancerous tumor.

LOUIS: I see it! Astounding!

JANE: Hopefully the same principle will apply. Also, it will be essential to find a way for chemotherapy to concentrate directly on the tumor or the cancerous region. The entire body will be affected by the chemo, but the potency of the drug will be aimed at the cancer cells.

LOUIS: I imagine the treatment will result in extreme fatigue. Maybe even an unconscious state.

JANE: That is possible, although the length of time of the treatment will be adjusted to take the patient's physical strength into consideration.

LOUIS: But if your theory is valid, Jane, chemo can be used for many kinds of cancer—

JANE: Because the destruction of the mitosis process would be the same in all cancer cells.

LOUIS: *(Gets excited.)* Leukemia, breast cancer, melanoma, lymphosarcoma, prostate cancer, Hodgkin's disease—! *(Doubles over in an extended coughing fit into his handkerchief. More blood.)*

JANE: Oh, Dad! I was afraid this might happen!

LOUIS: *(Still coughs.)* I am so… happy for you…

JANE: Dad, it is just a hypothesis. On paper it works, but—

LOUIS: It will work! It will work!

JANE: It will take months of testing and—

LOUIS: Of course! Of course!

JANE: And we can only guess at what the side effects will be—

LOUIS: Life! That will be the main side effect! *(Coughs again.)*

JANE: I shouldn't have said anything to you tonight, Dad. I should have waited until you were feeling better.

LOUIS: I couldn't wait that long. Besides, I wouldn't have missed this for anything in the world! My daughter! My Jane! *(Another coughing fit.)*

JANE: Let's get your coat on. *(Helps LOUIS with his coat.)* I'm hailing a taxicab and taking you home. Where's your hat?

LOUIS: Next to your nitrogen mustard!

JANE: *(Hands it to him.)* Here. Put it on. *(He does.)*

LOUIS: I can walk home from here—

JANE: It must be very cold by now. Listen to that wind! *(Takes off her lab coat and hangs it up.)* And it might be raining. *(Puts on her own overcoat and hat.)* You ought to have a scarf, Dad.

LOUIS: Scarfs suffocate me! *(Starts coughing as she takes him by the arm and leads him to the door.)* I can still walk, you know.

JANE: No one said you couldn't walk, Dad. But sometimes when you have a coughing fit, you do lose your balance—

LOUIS: Nonsense! *(Coughs and she braces him. He suddenly stops, serious.)* Jane, my dearest, you are going to save thousands—no, millions of lives.

JANE: *(Looks at him with tears in her eyes.)* If only I could save one special one. *(They EXIT as LIGHTS FADE to BLACK.)*

AFTERMATH

Louis Wright died of tuberculosis the next year and never saw chemotherapy perfected and widely used around the world. After testing by Jane Wright and a team of doctors at Harlem Hospital, the drug methotrexate was developed, which became the key to effective chemotherapy.

In 1964, Jane Wright was the only woman among the seven founders of The American Society of Clinical Oncology and was later the first woman elected as president of the New York Cancer Society. In 1967, she was appointed Associate Dean and Head of the Cancer Chemotherapy Department at New York Medical College. She also traveled the world, particularly Africa, establishing cancer clinics. Wright received many honors, awards, and citations during her life. Her husband, David Jones, a lawyer active in Black youth programs, died prematurely in 1976 from heart failure. Wright retired in 1986 and returned to art, painting watercolors until her death in 2011 at the age of 93.

NO MORE BIRDSONG
(1962)

BACKGROUND

Rachel Carson (1907-1964) was a popular author of nature books and a pioneer in the environmental movement that brought global awareness to the dangers of pesticides. She was born in rural Pennsylvania and began her career as a marine biologist for the U.S. Bureau of Fisheries. When Carson turned to writing about nature, she published two bestsellers: *The Sea Around Us* (1951) and *The Edge of the Sea* (1955). When the U.S. Department of Agriculture began using synthetic pesticides to destroy gypsy moths in 1957, Carson became active in the movement to control or stop the use of chemicals to kill pests. Working with the National Audubon Society and other groups, she researched the effects of the pesticides on the environment during a four-year project, which resulted in the book *Silent Spring*. While writing the book, Carson was diagnosed with breast cancer.

CHARACTERS

RACHEL CARSON (F) ....author and environmentalist
RUTH* (F) ....young nurse
MARIE RODELL (F) ....Rachel's literary agent
SIDNEY ROSS* (M) ....lawyer

*Fictional characters

SETTING

Time: September 20, 1962.
Place: A hospital room in Washington, D.C.

SET DESCRIPTION

The hospital room includes a bed, a bedside table with a telephone, and two chairs. There is one door into the room.

PROPERTIES

Thermometer, blood pressure monitor on wheels, wristwatch, stethoscope (RUTH); purse, files (MARIE); briefcase filled with papers (SIDNEY).

SOUND EFFECTS

Telephone ringing.

No More Birdsong

LIGHTS UP on Rachel's hospital room. RUTH helps RACHEL into the bed. RUTH wears a nurse's uniform, and RACHEL wears a hospital gown. RACHEL is unsteady and breathing heavily.

RACHEL: I really think I can manage—

RUTH: Please, Miss Carson. You are very weak. I don't want you to fall. *(Gets her onto the bed.)*

RACHEL: I'm not all that sick. Just… *(Settles into a sitting position.)* …very tired.

RUTH: Those chemo treatments take a lot out of a person. Do you feel like you just ran around the block?

RACHEL: More like I just ran a marathon!

RUTH: That's the feeling. You'll rest here for tonight, and by tomorrow, you'll feel strong enough to go home.

RACHEL: Until the next treatment.

RUTH: Until the next treatment. *(Takes a thermometer from her pocket and shakes it.)* Let me place this under your tongue, Miss Carson. *(Does so, then feels her forehead.)* You don't feel like you're burning up. That's good. Some patients seem to catch on fire. *(RACHEL mumbles.)* No talking. Not yet. I have to tell you, Miss Carson, I loved your books. Especially the first one, *The Sea Around Us.* Not that I didn't like the second one. Oh, they were both wonderful! Are you working on another? *(RACHEL mumbles again.)* Oh, don't answer that yet. *(Looks at watch.)* Times up. *(Takes the thermometer out and looks at it.)* Normal. That's good.

RACHEL: Thank you, and yes.

RUTH: What's that, Miss Carson?

RACHEL: Thank you for liking my books, and yes, I am working on another. Or was working on it. It's finished and is supposed to come out next week.

RUTH: *(Puts the blood pressure cuff on RACHEL'S arm.)* I'm going to take your blood pressure now that you've stopped huffing and puffing. A new book! Why, that is good news! *(Takes Rachel's blood pressure.)* What's this one called?

RACHEL: *Silent Spring.*

RUTH: What a pretty title. *(Finishes taking her blood pressure.)* A little high but nothing to be alarmed about. What does it mean, *Silent Spring*? Why is the spring so silent? *(Removes the cuff.)*

RACHEL: All is quiet because there is no birdsong.

RUTH: Last thing. I need to feel your pulse. *(Takes RACHEL'S wrist with one hand and checks her watch on the other.)* No singing birds? Why's that?

RACHEL: Because they're all dead. Killed by DDT, along with other wildlife and several plant species.

RUTH: My goodness, your pulse is racing!

RACHEL: I'm not surprised. You've hit a nerve, Miss…?

RUTH: Ruth. I should say so. What is this DDT thing? I've never heard of it.

RACHEL: Most Americans haven't. That is why I wrote the book.

RUTH: It sounds like some kind of poison.

RACHEL: It is. DDT is a chemical pesticide that is intended to kill gypsy moths and other farm pests, but when not used carefully, it pollutes the ground and water and ends up killing all kinds of animal and plant life.

RUTH: That's terrible! The government ought to stop it.

RACHEL: The U.S. Department of Agriculture promotes DDT and even supports the chemical companies that manufacture it! But the government makes no effort to supervise or control the use of such pesticides.

RUTH: No wonder your pulse went crazy. It makes my blood boil! So, Miss Carson, this new book of yours—*Silent Spring*—it's all about this DDT and what it does?

RACHEL: Yes. DDT and other insecticides like heptachlor and chlordane.

RUTH: Good for you, Miss Carson. *(Pause.)* Wait a minute. You said it is "supposed to come out next week." What did you mean by that?

RACHEL: There are… complications. My agent is working on— *(MARIE RODELL opens the door and pokes her head IN.)*

MARIE: Am I allowed to come in yet?

RACHEL: Marie!

MARIE: *(ENTERS carrying a purse and files.)* There was no one at the nurses station, so I thought—

RUTH: I'm just finishing up, ma'am. Miss Carson is allowed to have visitors now.

MARIE: Finally! I've been waiting down in that cafeteria. *(To RUTH.)* Do you know they have the worst coffee in all of Washington, D.C.?

RUTH: Yes, ma'am. I know. That's why I bring my own from home.

RACHEL: Marie, this is Ruth. She says my pulse is going crazy.

MARIE: I could have told you that!

RACHEL: Ruth, this is Marie Rodell, my literary agent and emotional bodyguard.

RUTH: Pleased to meet you, ma'am. I've got to go now. You stay in bed and rest, Miss Carson. And you, Miss Rodell, you get that book of Miss Carson's published next week—complications or no complications. Good day to you both. *(EXITS, pushing the blood pressure monitor.)*

MARIE: My, she certainly seems well-informed!

RACHEL: She liked my first two books.

MARIE: Well, the new one will make her hair stand on end.

RACHEL: If she gets to read it. If anyone gets to read it.

MARIE: Rachel, it's not like you to take a defeatist attitude! Where's your usual gumption?

RACHEL: I think the chemo kills more gumption than cancer cells.

MARIE: You poor dear. You must be exhausted! I shouldn't be here at all, and you should be sleeping.

RACHEL: I don't feel sleepy. Just… tired. Besides, I want to hear what Paul had to say. You did see him yesterday in Boston, didn't you?

MARIE: *(Hesitates.)* I did…

RACHEL: What did he say? Are they releasing *Silent Spring* next week or not?

MARIE: I couldn't quite get Paul to…

RACHEL: To what?

MARIE: To say yes or no. He was… ambivalent.

RACHEL: My own editor, the amazing Paul Brooks, has lost faith in the book.

MARIE: I wouldn't say that, Rachel, dear. But this lawyer from Houghton Mifflin had just been to see him, and poor Paul looked dazed.

RACHEL: Lawyers can do that. Maybe if I spoke to Paul on the phone—

MARIE: I wouldn't do that, Rachel. Not yet.

RACHEL: Not yet? Marie, the book comes out in a week! What are we waiting for?

MARIE: Paul promised me that he would talk to the publisher at Houghton. I think we should be patient.

RACHEL: It's a good thing Ruth is not taking my blood pressure right now! I'd break her machine!

RUTH: *(RUTH sticks her head IN.)* Miss Carson?

MARIE: Perfect timing!

RUTH: There's a man here to see you. I don't know if you want two visitors at once...?

RACHEL: Did he say who he is, Ruth?

RUTH: He did, Miss Carson. Sidney Ross. From Houghton Mifflin, he says.

RACHEL: I don't know any Sidney Ross from—

MARIE: And how would anyone from Houghton know you were here?

RACHEL: Unless...

MARIE: *(Realizes.)* Oh no! The lawyer!

RUTH: Should I let him in?

MARIE: No!

RACHEL: *(At the same time.)* Yes!

MARIE: Rachel, I don't think—

RUTH: He seems like the kind of man who's mighty determined to see Miss Carson.

MARIE: All the more reason—

RACHEL: Send him in, Ruth. *(To MARIE.)* I can handle this, Marie.

RUTH: I'll bring him in, but he can't stay long. You need your rest, Miss Carson.

MARIE: Tell him five minutes! *(RUTH EXITS.)*

RACHEL: You don't have to stay, Marie—

MARIE: I'm not budging. On anything.

SIDNEY: *(ENTERS wearing a three-piece suit and carrying a briefcase.)* Excuse me for bothering you while you're in the—

RACHEL: You're excused.

SIDNEY: I'm Sidney Ross from the legal department at—

RACHEL: So I've been told.

SIDNEY: I spoke with your editor Paul Brooks yesterday in Boston—

RACHEL: And now you're here. How industrious of you, Mr. Ross. It must be important.

SIDNEY: Well, you might say it is.

RACHEL: I just did.

SIDNEY: Ah, yes. *(Opens the briefcase and takes out files of papers.)* Since *The New Yorker* ran excerpts from your book *Silent Spring*, some legal difficulties have arisen.

MARIE: Legal difficulties? That sounds like a polite way of putting very bad news.

SIDNEY: Ah... yes. *(Pulls out one paper.)* Three days ago, the Dupont Chemical Company—

RACHEL: The manufacturers of DDT.

SIDNEY: Ah... yes. The Dupont Chemical Company has threatened legal action against *The New Yorker*, Houghton Mifflin, and the National Audubon Society.

MARIE: Why not the Girl Scouts of America?

SIDNEY: *(Looks at the papers.)* No, I don't think that organization is mentioned—

RACHEL: It was a joke, Mr. Ross. Go on.

SIDNEY: Oh... I see. *(To MARIE.)* The Girl Scouts. Very funny. *(Turns to another paper.)* The Velsicol Chemical Company—

RACHEL: *(To MARIE.)* They make the chlordane and heptachlor. Terrible stuff. It takes decades to break down.

SIDNEY: It seems Velsicol is planning to take similar action on the same three organizations.

MARIE: And on what grounds are these legal threats made, Mr. Ross?

SIDNEY: Grounds? Oh, grounds... *(Turns to another paper.)* That's on this page... Here it is. "Questionable documentation, insufficient evidence, lack of long-term study—"

RACHEL: That is quite enough, Mr. Ross. These are old arguments, all of which have been addressed before the U.S. Department of Agriculture and the Food and Drug Administration.

MARIE: So why exactly are you here, Mr. Ross?

SIDNEY: Exactly? Well... ah... to tell you that the legal department of Houghton Mifflin has advised the president of the company and Mr. Brooks not to release *Silent Spring*.

MARIE: Legal advice!

RACHEL: And have they taken your legal advice?

SIDNEY: Oh, I really can't say, but Mr. Brooks wanted you to know the situation.

RACHEL: It seems like Mr. Brooks could have simply called me on the phone and— *(SOUND EFFECT: PHONE RINGS.)*

MARIE: Right on cue.

RACHEL: *(Picks up the phone.)* Hello? *(Beat.)* Paul!

MARIE: Speak of the devil.

RACHEL: So nice of you to send Mr. Ross down here to enlighten me! *(Listens.)* What?

MARIE: What have they decided?

RACHEL: I see... *(Listens.)* Well, I say... *(Listens.)*

MARIE: *(Worried.)* Oh...

RACHEL: Yes... *(Listens.)* Really? *(Listens.)* You don't say! *(Listens.)* Oh, I understand. No, go ahead and take the other call. You've told me plenty, Paul. Thank you so much! *(Hangs up the phone.)*

MARIE: *(Puzzles.)* Thank you so much?

RACHEL: Yes. It seems Supreme Court Justice William Douglas called the president of Houghton Mifflin and encouraged him to publish *Silent Spring*, even if he has to fight the chemical companies all the way to his court! He read *The New Yorker* excerpts and is behind us one hundred percent.

MARIE: Oh, Rachel! *(Hugs her.)*

RACHEL: And not only that, *Silent Spring* is the October selection for the Book of the Month Club!

MARIE: Dupont and Velsicol will be furious! *(Laughs with RACHEL.)*

SIDNEY: My... this is certainly an interesting turn of events.

MARIE: Look at it this way, Mr. Ross. You might end up arguing a case in front of the Supreme Court!

SIDNEY: Oh, gosh... *(LIGHTS FADE to BLACK.)*

AFTERMATH

Silent Spring was released by Houghton Mifflin on September 27, 1962, and the book became a bestseller, making millions of Americans aware of the dangers of pesticides. Despite attacks from chemical companies, a movement for safer use of pesticides began, resulting in the formation of the U.S. Environmental Protection Agency.

Rachel Carson's cancer spread, and she died of a heart attack in 1964 at the age of 56. Carson was posthumously inducted into the National Women's Hall of Fame in 1973. In 1980, she was awarded the Presidential Medal of Freedom by President Jimmy Carter. Today, there are many parks, nature reserves, wildlife refuges, research institutes, science awards, structures, and schools named in her honor.

MAGIC RINGS
(1982)

BACKGROUND

The space probe Voyager 1 is the longest-operating spacecraft in the history of space exploration, having sent back to Earth thousands of photos of our solar system over a period of more than forty years. It was launched from Cape Canaveral, Florida, by the National Aeronautics and Space Administration (NASA) on September 5, 1977, and is currently the most distant object ever made by man, over 14 billion miles from Earth. The initial mission of Voyager 1 was to survey the outer planets in the solar system, not only flying near to them but also orbiting such rarely photographed planets as Jupiter and Saturn. The probe took photos of the planets, but also studied the weather conditions on them, measured their magnetic fields, and examined their moons. In January 1979, the probe reached Jupiter and began its observation phase of the largest planet in our solar system. In November 1980, Voyager 1 began its exploration of Saturn and its famous rings.

CHARACTERS*

WALTER BARRINGER (M).....retired science teacher; 84 years old
LOUISE WHITNEY (F).............nursing home attendant; 43 years old
KELLY (F) ....Walter's granddaughter; a 22-year-old college student

*ALL characters are fictional

SETTING

Time: A January afternoon in 1982.
Place: The lounge of a nursing home in Scranton, Pennsylvania.

SET DESCRIPTION

The lounge consists of a few comfortable armchairs and two smaller, easily-moved chairs. The room is sunny as light from the afternoon sun pours through the unseen windows.

PROPERTIES

Wheelchair, blanket, book, reading glasses (WALTER); copy of *National Geographic* magazine (LOUISE).

WALTER sits in a wheelchair, a blanket over his lap and legs, reading a book using thick reading glasses. He is dressed in a long-sleeve shirt, corduroy pants, and slippers. After a moment LOUISE ENTERS carrying a copy of *National Geographic* magazine. She is dressed in a light green uniform dress and sensible shoes.

LOUISE: There you are, Mr. Barringer. I thought you'd be in your room napping.

WALTER: *(Pleasantly.)* I already had my early afternoon nap. And it's too early for my late afternoon nap. You caught me between naps enjoying the sunshine here in the lounge.

LOUISE: Don't let that sunshine fool you. It's freezing outside. Only eighteen degrees when I started my shift.

WALTER: Louise, was that Fahrenheit or Celsius?

LOUISE: Now don't you go getting scientific on me again, Mr. Barringer. I'm not in your science class any more. Haven't been for some thirty years!

WALTER: So I daresay you've had plenty of time to forget the difference between Fahrenheit and Celsius.

LOUISE: No one uses Celsius after they get out of school. All I remember is there is a big difference between the two.

WALTER: Well put, Louise. If it were eighteen degrees Celsius outside it would be fine weather, and you could push me around the garden once or twice.

LOUISE: As it is, I think we'd both freeze to death by the time we got to the sundial! Look, Mr. Barringer. I brought you something. *(Hands him the magazine.)*

WALTER: *National Geographic.* I let my subscription lapse some time ago. Too many scantily-clad natives for a man my age!

LOUISE: *(Laughs.)* There's none of that in this issue!

WALTER: Too bad.

LOUISE: I found it in the reading room. It's almost six months old, but look at the cover!

WALTER: *(Happily.)* I don't need my reading glasses to recognize my old friend! Thank you, Louise!

LOUISE: I recognized it right away. Because of the rings. *(Points.)* See!

WALTER: Saturn's magic rings. Billions of little pieces of ice, droplets of water, and bits of rocks. All being pulled around the planet by a magnetic field. We think. I was a boy when I first saw Saturn in a picture book, and I knew that my fascination with the planet would never wane.

LOUISE: I didn't read the whole article. I mostly just looked at the pictures. But—

WALTER: *(Gets more excited as he pages through the magazine.)* Louise! Do you know what these are?

LOUISE: Uh... pictures of Saturn?

WALTER: These photos were taken by the space probe Voyager 1! In November of 1980 it got as close to Saturn as seventy-seven thousand miles!

LOUISE: That close?

WALTER: I saw some fuzzy pictures in the newspaper at the time, but these photos...! Look at them! As clear and detailed as photos of our moon. *(Points to a page in the magazine.)* And speaking of moons, here are Saturn's moons Tethys and Mimas. The photos are so clear you can see every crater and mountaintop! *(Turns the page.)* And look at this! The rift valley known as the Ithaca Chasma...! And here's the crater Herschel!

LOUISE: Steady, Mr. Barringer! Don't get overexcited or I'll have to get your heart medicine.

WALTER: Oh, Louise! Seeing these photos does my heart good. All my life I've studied Saturn and now I finally get to see her up close! I've lived long enough to actually see her, thanks to Voyager 1.

KELLY: *(ENTERS wearing a heavy winter coat, hat, and scarf. She is slightly upset and goes right up to WALTER.)* Grandpa! *(Relieved.)* I went to your room, but you weren't there, and I thought—!

WALTER: Kelly! What a surprise!

KELLY: I know your birthday party is tomorrow, but my ride back to college is leaving in the morning so I wanted to come by today to wish you a happy birthday! *(Kisses him on the cheek.)*

WALTER: I'm glad to see you any day, dearest. *(To LOUISE.)* Louise, this is my granddaughter Kelly. My youngest daughter's girl. Kelly, this is Louise Logan. I had her in science class back—

LOUISE: It's Louise Whitney now. I haven't been Louise Logan for over fifteen years, Mr. Barringer!

WALTER: Louise Whatever! She was in my science class. That's what counts. Louise has brought me a copy of *National Geographic* that has all the latest photographs of Saturn in it!

KELLY: That's your favorite planet, Grandpa!

LOUISE: Don't we all know it! Take off that heavy coat, dear. You'll roast in here. *(KELLY takes off her coat and tosses it on a chair.)* In class, we learned all the planets from your grandfather, but somehow Saturn got special attention.

KELLY: Because of the rings!

WALTER: The magic rings! You remember!

KELLY: How could I forget? All those cardboard planets hanging in your basement. Every time we came to visit, you had to show me your solar system. Especially Saturn.

WALTER: Of course!

KELLY: So Saturn became my favorite planet, as well. *(Sits in a chair near WALTER but speaks to LOUISE.)* In fifth grade I tried to make a cardboard model of Saturn for science class, but I couldn't figure out how to do the rings. So I went to Grandpa—

WALTER: Easy as pie. A paper plate with a big hole cut out of the middle!

KELLY: I think I still have it, somewhere deep in my closet at home.

LOUISE: You learned from cardboard planets, but that wasn't good enough in Mr. Barringer's class.

KELLY: What do you mean?

LOUISE: Can you believe this? Your grandfather marched the whole class out of the classroom and into the parking lot, where he drew these big chalk circles on the asphalt.

WALTER: Orbits, not circles.

LOUISE: Well, Mary McFee, she was the smartest girl in the class, you see. Your grandfather put her in the center of all the circles and told her she was the sun.

KELLY: Because she was the brightest student in the class! *(ALL laugh.)*

LOUISE: Exactly. But she had the easiest job because the sun never moved! Mary McFee just had to stand there! That didn't take brains!

WALTER: Mary McFee was the only fifth-grader who would stand still for a whole class. The rest of you were too wild!

LOUISE: Well, then he started assigning different students to different planets and told each one which circle—

WALTER: Orbit!

LOUISE: Which orbit to stand on. I remember Jonas Pendleton was Jupiter because he was so—

KELLY: Fat?

WALTER: No! Tall.

LOUISE: And poor Marie Marsinko was Pluto and had the biggest circle of all! After he assigned the planets, the rest of the students were moons and asteroids and comets and... who knows what else!

KELLY: What were you assigned, Louise?

LOUISE: That's just the thing. I was told I was Saturn and was pleased as punch! After all, I knew it was Mr. Barringer's favorite planet, so I felt kind of special. But then...

KELLY: Then?

LOUISE: Once I got to my circle— *(Catches herself.)* —my orbit, your grandfather handed me a hula hoop and said it was Saturn's rings. So I had to carry this big hoop around my waist for the rest of the class! I was mortified!

WALTER: I always used a hula hoop for Saturn. It was always the star of the show!

LOUISE: So the next thing he tells us is to walk our chalk line as if we were planets orbiting the sun. I was a bit chunky in those days—fat, actually—and there I was walking on my chalk line with this hoop around me, bumping into Jonas Pendleton and whoever was the planet on the other side of me—

WALTER: Uranus!

LOUISE: Ugh! Goofy Richard Castlemore! I remember now! And Jonas kept saying to me, "Louise Logan, if you bump me with that hula hoop one more time I'm going to twist it around your neck!" *(WALTER and KELLY laugh.)* And he would have, too!

KELLY: I always knew Grandpa must have been a fun teacher!

LOUISE: I wish they had someone like you, Mr. Barringer, teaching science at the middle school now. My son Ethan is getting lousy grades in science. He says it's boring.

KELLY: But science isn't boring!

WALTER: Spoken like a good granddaughter.

LOUISE: What are you majoring in at college, Kelly?

KELLY: Chemistry.

WALTER: She's going to be a doctor!

LOUISE: Good for you!

KELLY: Probably not a doctor. Maybe a nurse.

LOUISE: *(Laughs.)* Just don't end up working in a nursing home and having to deal with impossible old men like your grandfather!

WALTER: *(Cheerful.)* Your fifth grade class always was an ornery mob!

LOUISE: We sure were. Jonas Pendleton later served time for grand theft auto. *(To KELLY.)* But you've come here to see your grandpa and not me—even if I once played Saturn. I better get myself and my magic rings down to Mrs. Lytell's room before she wakes up and starts yelling for her massage. Nice meeting you, Kelly.

KELLY: And you too, Louise. Thanks for taking good care of my grandpa!

LOUISE: You just tell him to stop trying to teach me science after all these years! *(Laughs as she EXITS.)*

KELLY: Grandpa, how many times did you do that?

WALTER: Do what, Kelly?

KELLY: Have your students go outside and create the solar system.

WALTER: *(Thinks.)* Oh... a thousand times! *(They both laugh.)* I did teach forty-one years. Of course they hadn't invented the hula hoop when I first started teaching science. I don't remember what I used for Saturn.

KELLY: *(Pages through the magazine.)* These photos of Saturn are amazing!

WALTER: Taken by Voyager 1 last November. The closest any man-made object has ever gotten to my special planet.

KELLY: Wow!

WALTER: *(Smiles.)* Of course, I seem to remember Buck Rogers going to Saturn once.

KELLY: Who?

WALTER: Buck Rogers. In the Saturday morning movie serials. *(Laughs.)* I think he walked on Saturn's rings! In fact, I think he was chased on the rings by his nemesis Killer Kane! *(Laughs again.)*

KELLY: *(Laughs with him.)* On the rings? But that's impossible! They are made of bits of ice and—

WALTER: I know, I know! That's what made it so exciting!

KELLY: Even as a child you loved Saturn.

WALTER: Of course. But I'll tell what was more exciting than Buck Rogers.

KELLY: What?

WALTER: Well, I... *(Goes blank and stares ahead for a moment.)* I... *(A pause.)*

KELLY: *(Panics.)* Grandpa?!

WALTER: I... *(Suddenly comes back to life.)* Oh. Where was I?

KELLY: Are you alright, Grandpa? Should I call a nurse? Or Louise?

WALTER: *(Calmly.)* No, no. Just a little blackout. I get them sometimes. They are nothing.

KELLY: Are you sure?

WALTER: *(Alert.)* Now what was I saying?

KELLY: Something that was more exciting than Buck Rogers.

WALTER: Of course! It was in 1944. I was in the Navy. Somewhere in the middle of the Indian Ocean. But I heard the news all the same.

KELLY: What news?

WALTER: Scientists had been observing Titan for some time. You remember Titan?

KELLY: Saturn's largest moon.

WALTER: Exactly! In 1944 it was found out that Titan had the thickest atmosphere of any moon in the solar system. So thick that it showed bodies of water. Only Earth had such things! It made Saturn all the more magical to me.

KELLY: I didn't remember that.

WALTER: Six moons orbiting Saturn and those magic rings! It was far beyond Buck Rogers! *(Breathes deeply with excitement.)*

KELLY: *(Hugs WALTER.)* Oh, Grandpa! I love you! Still getting excited about Saturn after all these years! I'm so sorry I can't be here tomorrow for your eighty-fifth birthday. And I was too scatterbrained to get you a present because I just found out about my ride this morning. But I'll tell you what I'm going to do.

WALTER: What's that, Kelly?

KELLY: *(Gestures to the magazine.)* I am going to find a copy of that issue of the *National Geographic*, and I am going to frame the photos of Saturn for you. My roommate is an art major and she'll help me! I can hang them in your room. Would you like that?

WALTER: Of course I would, dearest.

KELLY: Great! *(Rises and puts on her coat.)* But I've got to run. I haven't even begun to pack, and my ride wants to leave at seven tomorrow morning. *(Hugs WALTER again.)* Happy birthday, Grandpa! I love you!

WALTER: I love you, too. And you have a good semester at school. Not too many parties! I know how chemistry majors like to mix their own drinks at parties! *(Both laugh.)*

KELLY: Goodbye, Grandpa! See you at spring break! *(EXITS quickly. WALTER looks again at the pictures in the magazine then stares at the sun through the unseen windows.)*

WALTER: The thickest atmosphere of any moon in the solar system... *(Goes blank and stares ahead like before.)* Imagine that. I... I... *(Has another blackout, but this one continues until eventually the LIGHTS FADE to BLACK.)*

AFTERMATH

On February 14, 1990, Voyager 1 reached the edge of our solar system and sent back photos of the whole system, a composition known as the Family Portrait. Eight years later it continued farther into space, surpassing the distance set by a previous probe, Pioneer 1. By 2012 the probe crossed the heliopause (the theoretical boundary where the sun's solar wind is stopped by the interstellar medium) and entered interstellar space, the region between stars. It is estimated that Voyager 1 will continue to travel through interstellar space until the year 2025, when its nuclear battery generators will no longer be able to provide the necessary energy for the electrical systems to operate the probe.

THE MILLENNIUM BUG
(1999)

BACKGROUND

As early as 1993, computer scientists started to alert the public about the impending Y2K, an acronym for the year 2000, and how it would affect computers worldwide. Most software systems were designed with the year in two digits, the dates usually expressed in MMDDYY (month/date/year) format. This meant that most computers had records of transactions with dates like 04/12/96. As the millennium approached, the realization that the year 2000 would be written as 00 meant that it would be indistinguishable from the year 1900. Information incorrectly dated 1900 would be inaccurate and possibly even destroyed. Near the end of the 1990s, panic set in as the fear of the "millennium bug" had companies, governments, and individuals worried about a total computer malfunction. In truth, many computer systems (such as all Mac programs) already used four digits for the year, and other systems would automatically adjust to the new century. But there were still many systems in danger, and over $330 billion was spent in the United States alone in the last years of the twentieth century to reprogram, replace, rewrite, and reinvent both hardware and software.

CHARACTERS*

EMILY PARSONS (F) .... young astronomy student
JUDITH KELLER (F) .... associate professor
　　　　　　　　　　　　　　　　of astronomy
DR. BUDRIDGE (M) .... professor of astronomy

*ALL characters are fictional

SETTING

Time: 11:55 p.m. on December 31, 1999.

Place: A planetarium in the science building of a state college in the American Midwest.

SET DESCRIPTION

The control desk for the planetarium is CENTER and has two stools behind it so the operators are facing the audience. The control panels and various switches are hidden from the audience by a ledge at the front of the desk.

PROPERTIES

Briefcase (BUDRIDGE).

SOUND EFFECTS

Mechanical whirring sounds.

LIGHTING EFFECTS

Stars.

The Millennium Bug

LIGHTS UP on the planetarium. JUDITH KELLER and EMILY PARSONS sit on stools and examine the control panels.

EMILY: Everything looks okay so far.

JUDITH: It's still five minutes 'til midnight.

EMILY: *(Laughs.)* And the end of the world!

JUDITH: Emily, don't tell me you believe all that Y2K hysteria!

EMILY: Not one bit, Professor Keller. *(Laughs.)* But the things you hear on TV! People are going crazy!

JUDITH: Some people. Not anyone who really understands computers like you do, Emily.

EMILY: My Aunt Faye believes that every computer in the world is going to blow up with the arrival of the year 2000! And my aunt doesn't even own a computer!

JUDITH: Yes, a lot of panic over nothing. What program are you in, Emily?

EMILY: WS1, the Winter Solstice Star Show. It's the one we use for middle school groups.

JUDITH: That's extensive enough. We ought to see any problems that arise with that program, I suppose.

EMILY: I can bring up AST 101, the program we use for the beginning astronomy class.

JUDITH: No, too many variables there. We'd have difficulty spotting problems.

EMILY: I know all these programs by heart, Professor Keller. If even one star or planet or moon is wrong—

JUDITH: *(Laughs.)* I believe you, Emily! I wish I had your photographic memory. And your young eyes.

EMILY: I just meant—

JUDITH: It's all right, Emily. You've been coming here to volunteer since… why, since your freshman year.

EMILY: Actually, my senior year of high school.

JUDITH: I had forgotten! And here you are on New Year's Eve.

EMILY: It was my idea! *(DR. BUDRIDGE ENTERS wearing an overcoat, muffler, and hat, and carrying a briefcase.)*

BUDRIDGE: *(Grouses.)* Judith! *(JUDITH rises, surprised.)* I thought I heard voices in here! Whatever are you up to?

JUDITH: Dr. Budridge! You gave us such a fright! I might ask what you're doing here so late.

BUDRIDGE: I asked first.

JUDITH: *(Goes to BUDRIDGE.)* Well, it's just about midnight and... well...

EMILY: *(Rises.)* We wanted to see if the millennium bug got to the planetarium computer!

BUDRIDGE: Millennium bug! Such nonsense! Miss...?

EMILY: Emily Parsons, Dr. Budridge. I was in your Physics 2 class.

BUDRIDGE: Physics 2. Well, in that class did I ever once consider the existence of a... a... millennium bug?

EMILY: No, but I took your class three years ago. We've only known about the millennium bug since—

BUDRIDGE: Judith, honestly, why are you here in the middle of the night looking for—?

JUDITH: It's New Year's Eve, Dr. Budridge. In another minute or two, it will be a new century. Emily has volunteered to be here with me so we can see what reaction the year 2000 will cause in the computer that runs the planetarium star presentations.

BUDRIDGE: Computers! It's just a star show used to illustrate the heavens!

JUDITH: But it's run by a computer. And as you know, it's not on the same computer system as the rest of the college.

BUDRIDGE: Don't I know that! Those fellows in computing sent me a couple of salesmen last spring. Said they could reprogram or rewire or something to the planetarium computer so it could figure out the correct year! Ridiculous! And they wanted to charge ten thousand dollars! The dean said it would have to come out of my S and E budget!

EMILY: S and E?

JUDITH: *(To EMILY.)* Services and Equipment. *(To BUDRIDGE.)* That's terrible!

BUDRIDGE: I'll say. Do you know how many grad assistants I can get for ten thousand dollars?

JUDITH: So, where did you get the money?

BUDRIDGE: What money?

JUDITH: To reprogram the computer.

BUDRIDGE: Why would I want to reprogram the computer? The star show works fine. It doesn't care if it's 1999 or 1937 or *2001: A Space Odyssey*! It's a star show, not a clock!

JUDITH: *(Looks at the control panel.)* Oh, dear...

EMILY: *(Also notices the control panel.)* Wow...

BUDRIDGE: *(To JUDITH.)* What are you two frowning about?

JUDITH: Well, Dr. Budridge, we may have a problem.

EMILY: I'll say...

JUDITH: Why don't you take off your coat and hat and come over here to the console?

BUDRIDGE: I'm in no hurry. *(Puts down the briefcase and takes off his coat and hat.)* The only reason I'm here so late is because the missus is having a New Year's Eve party at the house. I hate those parties! Told her I had a few things to do at the office. I thought if I waited until after midnight, most of the guests would be gone.

JUDITH: *(Points to her stool.)* Please sit here, Dr. Budridge.

BUDRIDGE: If you say so, Judith.

JUDITH: Emily, start the WS1 program.

EMILY: *(Returns to her stool.)* Yes, Professor Keller.

JUDITH: Lights down to one quarter. That ought to be dark enough. *(Stands behind the console between the two stools.)*

EMILY: Okay. *(LIGHTS DIM.)* Starting WS1. *(SOUND EFFECT: ELECTRONIC WHIRRING SOUNDS.)*

JUDITH: We're going to bring up the winter solstice sky, Dr. Budridge.

BUDRIDGE: Fine, fine... *(Slowly, the room is filled with LIGHTING EFFECT: STARS.)*

JUDITH: Ah, there it is!

BUDRIDGE: It's beautiful!

JUDITH: What time is the computer showing, Emily?

EMILY: Thirteen seconds to midnight. Should I start to rotate the stars, Professor Keller?

JUDITH: No. Let it stay just as it is. Don't make any adjustments. In fact, Emily, don't touch anything.

EMILY: Yes, Professor. *(Pause.)* Seven... six... five... four... three... two... one... Happy New Year! *(Suddenly, all the STARS go OUT as LIGHTS UP FULL.)*

BUDRIDGE: What just happened?

JUDITH: I'm not sure yet, Dr. Budridge. Emily, what time does the computer say?

EMILY: It's all blank. No power at all.

JUDITH: Try rebooting.
EMILY: Okay.
BUDRIDGE: It's not a power failure. The lights in the room are on.
JUDITH: They are on their own circuit, but the computer controls the level. When the computer went dead, the lights just went back to normal.
BUDRIDGE: Don't say dead!
EMILY: Rebooting...
JUDITH: Any luck?
EMILY: Yes! It's warming up! I can see each program coming back one by one!
JUDITH: That's a good sign.
BUDRIDGE: Of course, it is.
JUDITH: What date and time does the computer give?
EMILY: It's acting very weird...
BUDRIDGE: Weird? Young lady, that is not a valid scientific observation!
JUDITH: What is it doing, Emily?
EMILY: Well, Professor, the day is right, and the time reads 12:03, but the year is weird—I mean, strange. The numbers are racing by so fast I can't read them!
JUDITH: Let me see, Emily. *(EMILY gets off the stool and JUDITH sits.)*
EMILY: See what I mean?
JUDITH: The counter is going from zero-zero to 99 then repeating the sequence over and over again.
EMILY: It's trying to find the year, but it can't!
JUDITH: I think you're right, Emily.
BUDRIDGE: Forget the year. Let's see if the star show still works.
JUDITH: Certainly, Dr. Budridge. *(To EMILY.)* Where's WS1?
EMILY: *(Points.)* Right there, Professor Keller.
JUDITH: Let's give it a try. Lights down to one quarter. *(LIGHTS DIM.)* Starting program WS1... *(SOUND EFFECT: ELECTRONIC WHIRRING SOUNDS, then slowly the room is filled with LIGHTING EFFECT: STARS.)*
BUDRIDGE: Ah! There she is! What did I tell you? *(Rises.)* Where's my hat and coat? *(Chuckles.)* It's a star show, not a clock! *(Puts on his coat then hat.)*

EMILY: *(Hesitates.)* Uh... Professor Keller...
JUDITH: Yes, Emily?
EMILY: *(Looks up at the sky.)* Something's wrong...
BUDRIDGE: Wrong? *(Looks all around.)* It looks beautiful.
JUDITH: The computer clock has finally stopped spinning. It now says the year is zero-zero.
BUDRIDGE: Well, it fixed itself! Good going!
JUDITH: I'm not sure about that...
EMILY: *(Continues to gaze at "the sky.")* It's gone... It's not there!
BUDRIDGE: What's not there?
EMILY: Pluto.
JUDITH: Are you sure, Emily?
EMILY: Positive. *(Points.)* It should be right over there, but it's... gone.
BUDRIDGE: Well, I never thought Pluto was a legitimate planet, anyway. Just a mass of hot gasses.
EMILY: Where did it go, Professor?
JUDITH: I have a hunch. The computer year is zero-zero. It thinks it's 1900. Pluto was not discovered until 1930.
EMILY: That means—
JUDITH: That means every star, planet, moon, asteroid, comet... entire galaxies discovered since 1900 are no longer here.
BUDRIDGE: Nonsense! What kind of computer would know that?
EMILY: One that caught the millennium bug? *(LIGHTS FADE to BLACK.)*

AFTERMATH

The year 2000 arrived with relatively few mishaps, thanks to an estimated $200 billion spent worldwide to prepare computers for the new millennium. Though there had been anxiety across a wide range of industries—from banking and transportation to power plants and utilities—the costly preparations were mostly successful, and the programs that were expected to switch over to the new century did so without incident. Curiously, the United States detected missile launches in Russia but attributed them to the Y2K bug. However, there was no computer malfunction. The missile launches were real, part of Russia's war with Chechnya Republic.

While some fanatics had predicted that the millennium bug was a sign of the end of the civilized world, for many it was soon forgotten, turned into a New Year's Eve joke, or dismissed as a hoax. Some have already pointed out that a new "bug" will appear in the year 9999 when the computers will not be able to handle a five-digit year with the arrival of 10000.

MODERN MEDICAL ADVICE
(2021 AD/391 BC)

BACKGROUND

The Greek physician Hippocrates (c. 460 - c. 370 BC) is considered the "father of Western medicine." He was the first to practice healing through practical and analytical methods instead of through philosophy or religion. The son of a physician, he was born on the Greek island of Kos off the coast of present-day Turkey. Hippocrates studied the medical practices of the time, then began teaching the art of healing in a radical new way. He believed that disease was not caused by evil spirits or punishment from the gods but by natural causes and should be treated with natural methods. Hippocrates observed his patients thoroughly, talking with them about their lifestyle and what symptoms they were experiencing. He often preferred the use of liquids, rest, and mild herbs over powerful drugs and primitive medical procedures.

CHARACTERS

DR. CARLOTTA VEGA* (F) ...... modern-day general practitioner
MATTHEW SHIRE* (M) .... Dr. Vega's patient
HIPPOCRATES (M) .... mature physician and medical teacher
KYRIA KORRINA
    FLOROS* (F) .... Hippocrates's patient

*Fictional characters (Note: "Kyria" translates as "Mrs.")

SETTING

Time: Two different Tuesday mornings, one in September 2021 AD and the other in 391 BC.

Place: An examining room in Dr. Vega's office in Cleveland, Ohio, and an examining room at Hippocrates's medical school on the Greek island of Kos.

SET DESCRIPTION

The stage is divided in two. RIGHT is a modern doctor's office with a patient's examining table, a chair, and a stool on wheels. LEFT is a simple stone room in the classic Greek style with a stone bench with a cushion on it. The action in each room is simultaneous and LIGHTS remain UP on both scenes throughout.

PROPERTIES

Modern blood pressure monitor, stethoscope, brochure (DR. VEGA).

Modern Medical Advice

LIGHTS UP on the two separate doctor's offices, past and present. At LEFT, KYRIA KORRINA FLOROS sits on the bench. HIPPOCRATES stands next to her, holding her wrist and feeling her pulse. At RIGHT, MATTHEW SHIRE sits on the examining table as DR. CARLOTTA VEGA sits on the stool and takes his blood pressure. There is silence for a while as the two physicians concentrate.

DR. VEGA: *(Takes the cuff off his arm.)* A little high, Mr. Shire.

HIPPOCRATES: Your pulse is a bit fast, Kyrie Floros.

MATTHEW: I knew it!

KORRINA: Oh, dear!

MATTHEW: When that nurse took my blood pressure ten minutes ago, she said it was high.

DR. VEGA: I know. That's why I checked it again.

HIPPOCRATES: A rapid pulse is nothing to be upset about. It is probably caused by your worries about your stomach.

MATTHEW: Great! Now on top of everything else, I have high blood pressure!

DR. VEGA: The measurement is just a little high, Mr. Shire, not enough to be considered high blood pressure.

KORRINA: Master Hippocrates, my stomach is a constant worry to me! And now you say there is something wrong with my pulse! What is a pulse?

HIPPOCRATES: It is the speed in which blood is going through your body. It varies from time to time. When you sleep, for example, it slows down. But when you are upset, it goes a little faster.

MATTHEW: *(Worked up.)* I come here about my stomach, and now I learn I have high blood pressure! Maybe you should put me on blood pressure meds.

DR. VEGA: *(Calms.)* We don't know that you regularly have high blood pressure, Mr. Shire, so I'm not prescribing any meds for it today.

HIPPOCRATES: Kyrie Floros, try to relax. Tell me about yourself. I have never met you before.

DR. VEGA: You are a new patient here, Mr. Shire—

MATTHEW: The guy I had at the Morris Clinic retired! I couldn't believe it! He looked to me like he was only 50!

DR. VEGA: Well, now you are here. Tell me about yourself.

KORRINA: What is there to tell you? I am Korrina Floros. My husband is a magistrate. My children are grown up. Both married but no grandchildren.

HIPPOCRATES: That must be a great disappointment to you, but they must still be young.

KORRINA: That is no excuse, I tell them. I should have grandchildren!

HIPPOCRATES: What about you, Kyrie Floros? What is your life like?

MATTHEW: Not much to tell. I'm a broker. Stock investments. Financial planning. A little speculation once in a while.

KORRINA: I manage the household, supervise the servants, plan the meals, choose the menu for social occasions. We have many such gatherings because my husband is a magistrate.

DR. VEGA: It sounds rather stressful.

HIPPOCRATES: It must take a lot of responsibility on your part.

MATTHEW: It can be stressful. But I handle it.

KORRINA: It is what I have always done.

DR. VEGA: Are you married, Mr. Shire? Children?

MATTHEW: Married with two kids. A girl in college and a son on the couch.

DR. VEGA: He is not interested in stocks and money and such?

MATTHEW: Oh, he's interested in money all right. In spending mine!

HIPPOCRATES: You say your husband is a magistrate. He must be a very important man.

KORRINA: So he keeps telling me.

HIPPOCRATES: Does he suffer from any ailments? His stomach, for example?

KORRINA: Stamos Floros? He can eat anything! Our cook makes the most outrageous things, and he eats them! Fish with so many onions and peppers and marinated olives that you cannot taste the fish! Lamb that is swimming in a rich sauce of... I don't know what! He eats it, and he loves it! He has a stomach like a goat!

HIPPOCRATES: And you eat this food as well?

KORRINA: Of course! I don't know how to cook. I eat what he tells me.

Modern Medical Advice

DR. VEGA: What about your eating habits, Mr. Shire? Who does the cooking in your household?

MATTHEW: My wife is an excellent cook, and she loves cooking, but she's a child psychologist, works all day, writes up reports all night, and never finds time. We eat out a lot now that restaurants are back open.

DR. VEGA: Would you say you eat at healthy restaurants?

MATTHEW: I don't know if they're healthy places or not, but they're expensive. My wife picks them.

DR. VEGA: But you have a choice of what you eat.

MATTHEW: Sure, I pick what I eat. I just eat too darn much. Maybe I need diet pills.

HIPPOCRATES: I think we should do something about the food you eat. That will help a great deal.

DR. VEGA: How long ago did these stomach pains begin, Mr. Shire?

HIPPOCRATES: When did you first notice these pains in your stomach, Kyrie Floros?

MATTHEW: I don't know exactly. A few months ago.

KORRINA: A long time ago. I was too afraid to tell my husband.

MATTHEW: My wife got fed up with me complaining about my stomach and made this appointment for me.

KORRINA: But one day last week, the pains were so bad I could not get out of bed in the morning. So, my husband found out.

MATTHEW: She says I probably have ulcers.

KORRINA: He says I have some evil thing within me.

DR. VEGA: Your blood tests from last week show nothing that would indicate ulcers.

HIPPOCRATES: There is nothing evil within you, Kyrie Floros.

DR. VEGA: And according to what you told the nurse, the pains do not come following a meal.

HIPPOCRATES: What is ailing your stomach is something from nature, not from evil spirits.

MATTHEW: I guess I'm just cursed with a bad stomach.

DR. VEGA: I don't believe in curses, Mr. Shire.

MATTHEW: Neither do I, Doc, but I gotta blame something.

HIPPOCRATES: Since your ailment comes from nature, the cure comes from nature. Kyrie Floros, do you get much exercise?

KORRINA: Exercise? What do you mean? Like the Olympic games? Me?

HIPPOCRATES: For example, did you walk here today?

KORRINA: I should say not. I came in my chair! What would my husband say if word got back to him that I was walking the streets of the town?

DR. VEGA: Mr. Shire, do you get much exercise?

MATTHEW: Me? I haven't got time!

HIPPOCRATES: You have a garden, I suppose?

KORRINA: Oh, yes! A beautiful garden! If I say so myself, it is the most beautiful on the island of Kos!

HIPPOCRATES: Is it large?

KORRINA: Indeed, it is!

HIPPOCRATES: Surely your husband would not object to your walking around the garden every day. Let us say, for 30 minutes?

DR. VEGA: You work at the Sullivan Building, I suppose.

MATTHEW: Sure do.

DR. VEGA: On what floor, Mr. Shire?

MATTHEW: Third. I have a corner office—

DR. VEGA: Instead of taking the elevator twice a day—

MATTHEW: Four times a day. I go out for lunch.

DR. VEGA: Even better. Walking up or down two flights of stairs four times a day will make a surprising difference.

MATTHEW: For my heart?

DR. VEGA: And your stomach.

KORRINA: Just walk around the garden for 30 minutes a day? The servants will think I am crazy!

HIPPOCRATES: You will be surprised at the difference it will make on your stomach.

MATTHEW: Maybe I just ought to join a gym or something.

DR. VEGA: Mr. Shire, do you know why there are so many of those gyms everywhere?

MATTHEW: People like to exercise?

DR. VEGA: People like to join them. After a month or two, most of them stop going.

MATTHEW: Then I'll get one of those exercise machines. Put it my bedroom.

DR. VEGA: After a month most people use them to hang wet towels on. Try the stairs.

HIPPOCRATES: You can make walking in the garden part of your daily routine.

KORRINA: How do you mean, Master Hippocrates?

HIPPOCRATES: For example, you say you have to plan the meals and the food for social occasions. I imagine you do this with the cook?

KORRINA: Yes! And it takes forever!

HIPPOCRATES: I suggest you tell the cook that she is to walk with you through the garden each day while you two discuss the meals.

KORRINA: Will she do that? *(Beat.)* But she's only the cook! I am mistress of the house. She will do it!

DR. VEGA: Of course, the very best exercise is walking. Do you get much opportunity for walking, Mr. Shire?

MATTHEW: When will I find time to walk?

DR. VEGA: After dinner. On weekends. Is your neighborhood a nice one for walking?

MATTHEW: The only people I see walking in my neighborhood are the ones walking their dogs.

DR. VEGA: Do you have a dog?

MATTHEW: Heck, no. My daughter has a cat that we are stuck with.

DR. VEGA: Did you know that people who own dogs are less stressed and have lower blood pressure readings than those without pets?

MATTHEW: I thought you said I didn't have high blood pressure!

DR. VEGA: I was thinking of your stomach.

KORRINA: Master Hippocrates, I am wary of many of the things you say. The physicians I have seen in the past do not talk like you do. They give me herbs. And potions. And recommend that I offer sacrifices to the gods.

MATTHEW: *(Gets testy.)* I'm not sure I like your new-fangled approach, Doc.

DR. VEGA: There is nothing new about it. My methods are very old. They go back to the teaching of Hippocrates in the third century BC.

KORRINA: *(Gets testy.)* I'm not sure I like these modern ways of yours!

MATTHEW: *(Stands.)* I'm a busy man! I've got pains in my stomach, and I've tried all that over-the-counter garbage and it doesn't do any good!

KORRINA: *(Stands.)* My husband is a busy man and won't put up with a wife who is sick in her stomach all the time!

MATTHEW: *(Shouts.)* I want prescription meds! Strong ones!

KORRINA: *(Shouts.)* I want powerful herbs and potions!

MATTHEW: And I want X-rays and biopsies and an MRI!

KORRINA: And I want to sacrifice a lamb to the gods!

MATTHEW: I want a stomach transplant!

KORRINA: Not a lamb. A cow! A bull! *(Silence as MATTHEW and KORRINA catch their breath. They then quietly sit back down with weariness. A long pause.)*

DR. VEGA: Are you finished, Mr. Shire?

HIPPOCRATES: Do you feel better, Kyrie Floros?

MATTHEW: I guess so...

KORRINA: I am so sorry...

DR. VEGA: *(Brightens.)* I recommend a diet that will not irritate your stomach, Mr. Shire. *(Hands him a brochure.)* This brochure is very helpful. A glass of red wine with dinner will help. So will exercise. And maybe a dog. Not a puppy. Give it six weeks. If you are still having pains, come back and see me again.

HIPPOCRATES: *(Brightens.)* I recommend that you eat simple things—vegetables, fruits, bread, a bit of wine. A soothing drink of water mixed with a little honey and vinegar. Try to find time in your life for walking. I will speak to your husband about these things, Kyrie Floros. And no lamb or cow or bull for the gods. They are overfed as it is. If you do not feel much better in six weeks, come back to me. *(Pause.)*

MATTHEW: Not a puppy?

DR. VEGA: Too stressful. Rescue a mutt that is at least a year old. *(LIGHTS FADE to BLACK.)*

AFTERMATH

Hippocrates taught and practiced medicine on the island of Kos until his death. He believed that most ailments would be cured by nature if allowed to take its usual course of action. He termed the point at which either the patient succumbs to the disease or nature brings about a cure as the "crisis." He was also active in treating patients where nature itself would not suffice. For example, he was one of the earliest physicians to reset bones with splints and traction. Although the methods were primitive, Hippocrates did perform surgery when necessary and even devised tubes to help internal organs function. Hippocrates's ideas, authored by himself and others who followed in his teachings, were collected into a work entitled *The Hippocratic Corpus*, which still serves as the foundation for modern medical practice today. As a testament to his contributions to modern medicine, physicians today still take the Hippocratic Oath, a statement of ethics regarding the practice of medicine. Varying records of Hippocrates's age at the time of death range from 80 to 100.

APPENDIX
Plays by Branch of Science

Play	Biology	Physics	Chemistry	Environmental Science	Astronomy	Mathematics	Engineering/Invention	Women in Science	Blacks in Science
Footsteps Around the World					X	X			
Miracle Glass		X					X		
Mirror Image Scribbling	X	X		X			X	X	
The Mad Prophet of Medicine	X		X						
And Yet It Moves		X			X	X			
To Frame My Face	X								
Noise		X					X		
Words and Wires		X					X		
No Wires		X					X		
The Train to Tuskegee				X					X
Little Curies	X	X					X	X	
King of the Universe			X		X			X	
Mold Juice	X		X						
Garage Guys							X		
The Movie Star and the Composer		X				X	X	X	
Decoding the Doll Woman						X		X	
Feeding the Enemy	X		X					X	X
No More Birdsong			X	X				X	
Magic Rings					X		X		
The Millennium Bug						X	X		
Modern Medical Advice	X								

ABOUT THE AUTHOR

THOMAS HISCHAK, who also wrote *Plays of the American Experience* for Meriwether Publishing, is the author of over 50 plays that have been produced across America, as well as in Great Britain, Canada, and Australia. His playwriting awards include the Stanley Drama Award (New York City) for *Cold War Comedy* and the Julie Harris Playwriting Award (Beverly Hills, California) for *The Cardiff Giant*. Hischak is also the author of over 30 books on theatre, film, and popular music, including *The Oxford Companion to the American Musical, The Rodgers and Hammerstein Encyclopedia, Broadway Plays and Musicals, Through the Screen Door, The Tin Pan Alley Encyclopedia, The Mikado to Matilda: British Musicals on the New York Stage, Word Crazy: Broadway Lyricists, American Literature on Stage and Screen, Theatre as Human Action, 1939: Hollywood's Greatest Year, The Oxford Companion to American Theatre,* and *The Oxford Companion to the American Musical.*

From 1983 to 2015, Hischak was Professor of Theatre at the State University of New York at Cortland, where he received such honors as the 2004 SUNY Chancellor's Award for Excellence in Scholarship and Creative Activity and the 2010 SUNY Outstanding Achievement in Research Award. Four of his books have been cited as Outstanding Non-fiction Books by the American Library Association, and *The Oxford Companion to the American Musical* was cited as an Outstanding Reference Work by the New York City Public Library in 2008. Hischak is a Fulbright scholar who has taught and directed in Greece, Lithuania, and Turkey. He is currently on the adjunct faculty of Flagler College, where he teaches courses on theatre and film.

PERFORMANCE APPLICATION

Unlimited amateur rights at a single location are granted with the purchase of this book. For performances at contests or other locations, a royalty fee of **$10 per play per performance** is due.

We hereby request permission to perform the plays listed below from ***Plays of Science & Invention*** by Thomas Hischak.

Play(s) being performed: _____

Number of performances: _____ Dates of production: _____

Name of producing organization: _____

Contact name: _____

Address: _____

_____

_____

Phone: _____

Email: _____

Amount due: _____

Payment: ☐ Check Enclosed ☐ Credit Card ☐ School PO# _____

Card number: _____

Expiration date: _____ Verification code: _____

Mail this application with your payment to:

MERIWETHER PUBLISHING
A division of Pioneer Drama Service, Inc.

PO Box 4267
Englewood, CO 80155-4267
or
Email to: payments@pioneerdrama.com